PRAISE FOR
THE PALACE OF LIGHT

"The Palace of Light: As you sense the shifts and experience the transformations within your life and the world at large, Lisa McCardle shares profound insights and practical guidance for navigating such salient times. Gleaned from her raw, yet transformative experiences, The Palace of Light provides channeled inspiration and touching stories, serving as a guiding light, reminding you that the turbulent times are your wake-up call to reconnect with yourself in grander and bolder ways."

> **- Karen A. Dahlman,** MA, published author, licensed professional counselor, spirit communicator, and host of Creative Visions TV

"I love the journey that I took through the Palace of Light. I can still recall and visualize and sense the divine path that supports the spiritual seeker. Words layered with emotion and beauty, my heart found this engaging and activating. I know this divine book will help anyone find their way home to themselves, their true sacred self with ease and grace."

- **Amanda Romania,** International author, intuitive, visionary spiritual mentor, teacher of metaphysics and is a Master Akashic Record Oracle

The Palace of Light is a soul filled journey of letting go and rising up. The tools within the pages are essential for each person walking on their spiritual journey at this time. The personal experience of ascension within its pages was heartfelt and profoundly beautiful. I felt as if I was walking alongside the author with each step of the journey home.

- **Lynn Kirkham,** Creator of *Yes, You Can Speak*, Speaking Coach

Palace of Light is a profoundly activating soul guide and memoir, written from the heart, for anyone along the spiritual ascension journey. While the ascension experience can be emotional and challenging, this book clears a pathway for extraordinary joy, personal discovery and life-changing soul-expansion. Lisa McCardle has created a cosmic love-gift for humanity within these pages, showing each of us how to walk the path home toward our greatest expression of love, light and higher consciousness.

- **Dr. Karin Luise,** Master Soul Coach and author of *The Fatherless Daughter Project* and *Sacred Shift*

The Palace of Light will take you on a journey like no other, walking the journey of deconstruction and ascension, rising up whole, holy and new. The story telling pulls you in, while the practical information and tools become a priceless road map to walk you home. This book is a must read for all those going through the journey of awakening on planet earth at this time.

- **Jessica Hidari,** Founder, Fem Talks, Feminine Frequency, <u>Spiritual Women Leaders Network</u> and Women of Color Wisdom Series

Lisa is here to guide us to greater amplification of light on earth. Her new book, The Palace of Light, is a must read. It will take you on an empowering journey to wholeness. Her story telling is captivating and engaging- while the practices and tools weaved in to support you on your path to a remembrance of your divine light.

- **Lauren Roxburgh,** The Body Whisperer, Author of *Taller, Slimmer, Younger* and *The Power Source.*

PALACE
OF
LIGHT

Finding Your Way Home

BY
LISA MCCARDLE

ISBN: 979-8-218-20135-7 (Paperback)

DEDICATION

I dedicate this book to Tim Sherman. Thank you for loving me through life and the great after. Thank you for being my greatest teacher and for standing by my side forevermore as a light of Spirit, purveyor of unconditional love, and my greatest cheerleader still. Thank you, Satchel Sherman, for teaching me about motherhood by becoming my son through soul contract and for bravely walking this journey home with me.

CONTENTS

Preface
The Beginning:
How I Disappeared

It is so hot, I can barely breathe. I actually think I might suffocate buried so deeply within these covers with just the tiniest of an air hole, barely big enough for the tip of my nose to poke through. I sleep here wrapped in my cotton cocoon, just like this, every night. Night after night, I tuck myself further and further away from the outside world and deeper into some kind of inner security. I am terrified.

I soothe myself thinking that if I can't see her, then maybe, just maybe, she can't see me. This works, until it doesn't.

In time, I throw the covers off and take a deep gasping breath of humid, stale, hot air, while still refusing to open my eyes. Another breath, then another. I slowly squint open one eye, my heart is pounding, tears are already forming in anticipation. And there she is, just as she always is, waiting for me.

If I had met her at a later point in my life, things would have been different. I perhaps would have understood why she was coming to me in the middle of the night. I might have been able to help her in some way through the veils of time.

She is beautiful really, both sassy and self-confident. Her wide-brimmed, red hat is twice as big as her petite face. Her red corset is sexy and somehow provocative, even from my four-year-old perspective. Her long legs cross delicately, as the frill of her dress cascades down around her sculpted ankles. She sits in wait.

I am frozen in the display of her incredible beauty.

She laughs at me, just as she always has, or at least that is my perspective. She really may just be overcome with joy to see me or perhaps BE seen by me. I scream, just as I always have, with blood-curdling intensity, as she sits there staring into my eyes, laughing at me.

As I am screaming and panting for breath, tears begin streaming down my face. My sweet, far-too-young mother comes bolting into my bedroom, just as she always has. She finds me shaking. I quickly point with my tiny hand and cry out, "Mamma, she's there again! The lady in the red dress, on top of my dresser! Look, Mamma, LOOK!" My mother takes me in her arms, with barely a glance over her shoulder in the direction of the dresser. "It is nothing, honey, there is nothing there," she whispers. Gone again is the lady in the red dress, at least for now.

This night was like many nights where my mother would explain away the images I saw or the voices I heard. "It must have been the light of a passing car casting a reflection on the wall." Or, "You must have been having a bad dream." Better yet, "Your imagination must be playing tricks on you."

This Lady in Red was just one of the many characters who would visit me on regular occasions, making gentle contact, yet leaving me confused, frightened, and completely unsure of what was real and what was not. Each encounter left me in wonder of the world I was witnessing and the world others seemed to dismiss. Playing through the veils of the shadows, I always found myself alone and confused.

In those moments, I began to clearly understand that these sorts of experiences were simply not understood, acknowledged, or welcomed in my home. They were quickly dismissed and put away, and I believed that if I was to be loved, then I must dismiss and put them all away, too.

This is how I disappeared.

I grew up in the countryside of Lancaster, Pennsylvania in a farmhouse built in the 1870s. The farmhouse, with a main house and several outbuildings, was once the stopover point between two towns. It was first a saloon, later a bed and breakfast. Its history was long and rich, and it was nestled within miles and miles of open cornfields.

In many ways, it was an exquisite experience being a kid on acres and acres of farmland with horses and so many outbuildings. Hours and hours were spent playing house and hide-and-seek. Endless creative imagination games kept my young mind entertained. Far too often, though, I was greeted with quick moving shadows and voices talking high above in the halo, resulting in the frequent, foreboding chills that crawled up my spine. They knew I could hear them, yet I had no idea what was happening.

I was raised in a religious household, and things such as ghosts and communication with the spirit world were strongly discouraged. From that perspective, these connections were "of the world," meaning "not of God," or worse yet, they were somehow "dark," perhaps even "evil." In fact, such things were certainly not to be any part of any reality in which we were living, especially not part of my own.

And so it began, the journey of deconstructing what I saw, what I heard, and what I had yet to understand. I dismissed and dismantled the truth of myself and silenced not only what I heard or saw but also what I thought, believed, and said. It seemed I just knew things, saw things, heard things, felt things. Even so, it was necessary to deny this part of myself. I did this by shutting hard against the doors of my own perception, connection, and otherworldly understanding.

I zipped myself up and blocked everything that wasn't able to be explained. I became the "good girl" so that I wouldn't rock the boat with weird outbursts, so that everyone else could find comfort and go back to sleep, for they had dismissed their superpowers many years before. A part of me then disconnected, disappeared, and went into a deep slumber with them. It would be more than twenty years before these gifts were re-activated, embraced, and eventually embodied.

You can't dismiss and deny one aspect of yourself without shutting down many of your other expressions. My "deconstruction" continued for the next fifteen years, taking on many different forms of denial, dismissal, and silencing of self. I even accepted abuse by others and myself, felt separation, lived in lack, hid myself, turned down my voice, and ultimately created a life of disconnection.

Why? Because I believed the lies.

They say that 90% of reality is our perception. I would go as far as to say that at least half of the perceived realities we have of ourselves, truth be told, are lies! All the parts that don't feel good definitely are. The great lie is that we are intended to struggle or to suffer, while leaving parts of ourselves out of the equation, in order to be loved. We have been programmed to believe that nothing good comes easy, "no pain, no gain," so they say. We work hard and climb our way to the top or settle for the hand life deals us, no matter how painful, because "that is life and just how life is." We simply believe the lies and have forgotten the truth.

My intention is to show you what you may not see so that you can see it clearly for yourself, so that you can remember what it is that you have forgotten. The truth is that you are an infinite being living in an infinite Universe. You are precious and whole, and it is time for you to find your way home, back to your birthright of knowing, connecting, shining your brightest light, and being sourced at your highest level.

What I want for you is to know, through every cell of your gorgeous self, is that there is much more than all of the lies you have been living. There is another way. It is right there already inside of you, humming right along the story you are currently living, just waiting to be sculpted and expressed in the wholeness of your truest light self.

I want for you to wake up in the morning with gratitude in your heart and curiosity in your head for all the miracles and magic the day has in store for you. I wish for you to be in the driver's seat of your extraordinary life, to feel sourced in the aspects that have the most meaning to you: in your relationships, your health, your money, your self-worth. I encourage you to find again, or for the first time, your truest power, forgiveness, abundance, gratitude, and love, truly tapping into your infinite soul-self, while expressing all through your greatest service.

I know this is possible for you because I have walked the journey myself. I have found the magic again! I died 1000 deaths to be reborn 1001 times, remembered. I was able to trust in and expand upon my own greatest gifts of seeing through the veils and receiving messages from Spirit, thus allowing the inspired words of this book to be gifted to you. I am now committed to walking myself and thousands of others just like you back home, back to the light and to the truth, so we can all be divinely guided and inspired. To be remembered. To create as the creators we are, each by our own unique and divine design.

The benevolent channeling in this book came through Spirit and a group who call themselves The Light Council with the intention of connecting you, the reader, to your greater knowledge. Their messages are enhanced and encoded for you to support your own journey of healing and connection, to awaken and allow your gifts to fully activate, and to align you with your purpose and ultimately your greatest service.

My journey of becoming a spirit channel started with an initiation from Quan Yin, the Goddess of Compassion. She began by funneling words through my consciousness. This all occurred effortlessly through me, as I was a young, twenty-seven-year-old yoga teacher at the time. I would have my students in savasana or corpse pose, and the words would gracefully flow through me. They were beautiful words and had a tone that was simply not my own, causing me to be in shock and simultaneously in awe.

Years later, I would meditate and allow the words to flow through me in written manuscripts, some of which I am sharing with you in these pages. Eventually, Quan Yin, along with one of my mentors, guided me, gradually and with much patience, on how to slide over so she could slide in. It was like I was stepping back from the center stage to sit in the balcony as an observer. This was when the full-body channeling began, which I experience, to this day, as being still and present but with words, frequency, and even tone as coming from a higher dimension.

My channeling then evolved. I moved from the angelic, ascended master realm into the galactic plane, and eventually The Light Council came in. It did take a few years to fully understand how to move out of the way to let the light of these sacred beings meld and move with my own.

The Light Council has been speaking through me now for several years. It began with a Pleiadian contact, as I carry Pleiadian starseed remembrance, and then moved quickly into connection with the entire council. The members present in different numbers, ranging from nine to thirteen, depending on the day and what is needed.

I see these beings as a council of pure light. I see, with my mind's eye, what you might consider to be a large roundtable with each member of the council appearing as a different frequency of light. There are some members of the council who I have not directly communicated with. They have explained this as being so since each of them holds a different star imprint, such as Pleiadian, Lumarion, Syrian, Arcturian, Atlantean, etc. The ones that I hold a remembered frequency with are the ones I communicate most directly with.

Mostly I hear their messages. At other times, I invite them to move into my body, using my frequency, voice, and hands to speak. They are always most gracious and grateful for this ease of access, and it leaves me feeling light, free, expanded, and deeply loved. You will learn more about these beings of light and receive their loving guidance as you proceed through these pages.

Their message for all of us is clear: "There has never been a greater time on planet earth to awaken your light. Rise up in your power, dearest ones, and walk the consciousness of humanity home to the Palace of Light."

LIGHT COUNCIL CHANNEL

"There is but one truth. You are an infinite being with limitless potential! All else is simply an illusion created through fear to keep you vibrating at one, one hundredth of your truest potential. It is time now to awaken fully to the ultimate truth of this infinite potential that is alive within you, not within a select few, but within each and every molecule of each and every being that is present here on this earthly plane.

The cloud of illusion that had blown through you some time ago is transmuting, the veil is lifting, and your consciousness is expanding along with your opportunity to vibrate from a frequency that is experienced as being entirely new. The truth is, although it feels different, it is truly your natural state of being, and therefore there is a resonance of "familiar" to it. Breathe it, live it, drink it, allow it to become normalized once again within you so that you, through your awakening, may remember the truth of who you ultimately are!

This journey of awakening is imminent, although each being is embracing it at a different frequency, the harmonization will come in time. Those who are "popping" through the veil first continue to hold the light upon the pathway so that those who are coming through behind may see clearly and find their way. Both are precious and fierce in the proclamation of the NEW.

We are in great honor and awe of each and every one of you. Though we never said it would be easy, we guarantee that you will be glad you parted the veil and rose up to the light."

~ The Light Council

Pillar One
PRESENCE

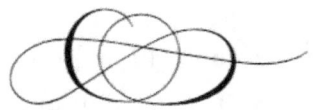

The Palace of Light
Finding Home

"Your hand opens and closes, opens and closes. If it were always a fist or always stretched open, you would be paralyzed. Your deepest presence is in every small contracting and expanding, the two as beautifully balanced and coordinated as birds' wings."

~ **Rumi**

I make a deal with the Universe. I promise that I will go to every single house that is available, even if I know one or another isn't for me, until my dream is made manifest. "Molding the clay" I call it. It's like dating. With each connection or exploration, you pull the pieces of what you most love, getting clearer on the pieces that are not part of the masterpiece creation. In time, you are molding your preferences into the perfect match.

For six months I search, pray, pause, wait, and show up. I find myself pondering an odd ad: "Large home on shared property. Another unit occupied by female." I tell myself that this could not possibly be my Palace of Light, so I ignore it. A few days later, I hear that all-too-familiar whisper, "You said you would look at everything." I recognize the reminder from my higher self in collaboration with the Universe itself, so I go.

As I walk through the door, the only thing I initially see is the insane mess of construction. I stumble through saws, scraps of wood, and dust, as I make my way through a very open and expansive floor plan and into a massive kitchen. I spot a hand-painted owl on tiles above the countertop. She is hiding behind a bunch of water bottles, towels, and lunch from yesterday. The owl has been potent medicine for me for many years, and I know that when one shows up in any form, it is summoning me to pay close attention. It is in this moment when I am able to see beyond the mess to the light streaming through the mass of windows, calling me toward one of the most spectacular, sweeping views I have ever seen.

It turns out that this palace checks every single box on my list of things I want in my new home, and so it is, we move into this amazing Palace of Light. On most days thereafter, for nearly four years, my partner Tim and I would look at each other and simply say, "Have I told you today how much I love this house and the life we have created?" We said it so often that it just became a nod and a "Have I told you today?" followed by our smiles.

I created this Palace of Light. I dreamt it into fruition, every last detail constructed within my heart many years before I ever walked through the front door. All of the details were etched within my dreams, each step was leading me home. "There will be light streaming in from all directions," I told myself as I dreamt out loud to the sky, my guides, the crows, my cat, and anyone else who was willing to listen. The skylights, sweeping views, and every last detail I manifested into reality.

Chapter One
Presence

"Always hold fast to the present. Every situation, indeed every moment, is of infinite value, for it is the representative of a whole eternity."

~ Johann Wolfgang von Goethe

The first and most fundamental step of the awakening process is seemingly simple, yet it seems to be phenomenally difficult in practice. *Presence.* Take an opportunity right now to close your eyes and give yourself the gift of absolute presence, just a minute or two of being still, following your breath, going inside, and focusing on the here-and-now moment. Set a timer. Ready? Set! Go!

Was that exhilarating or aggravating? What did you notice? Did your mind resist? Did it give you one hundred things that need to be done ASAP, remind you of calls you have forgotten, give you a cramp in your leg? Did you need to look at your phone? Presence is a word thrown around often, especially in the consciousness communities. Yet how do we actually embody the essence of what true presence really means?

Indeed presence is the greatest gift when embraced and then ultimately embodied. It is the alpha and the omega, the beginning and the end. It is the full circle experience of divine creation. The truth is that nothing else becomes as fully available to you as it would otherwise be until presence is understood and eventually mastered. After that, the next level comes in: *fierce presence.*

Presence is the initiation, the first step, the one that you will come back to time and time again. When you are exploring the future, you are riding through waves of anxiety. When gazing into the past, you are summoning a state of depression. Depression is the sensation of being pressed down upon, like a thumb held tightly on your pulse of existence. It feels like you can't breathe!

If you are driving in your car and spending 90% of your time looking in the rearview mirror, what would happen? Most likely you would crash. If you are spending all of your time looking at your GPS for the turns in the road five miles ahead, anticipating what might be there so you can be prepared, what would happen? Most likely you would crash. What gets you to your destination safely? Both hands on the wheel do. "Keep your hands relaxed and yet ready at two o'clock and ten o'clock, with your gaze just a few feet in front of you," I told my son when he was learning to drive. This is how you navigate your journey to any destination, with fierce and absolute presence.

Presence is the key to shifting and ultimately raising your frequency. There are times when fierce presence may come down to you tapping a hand on the table in front of you with an intense determination to Be! Here! Now! Other times you may tap on your thymus gland, the point on your sternum or chest bone, summoning the here and now into current time focus. Only in presence can you find the calm creator frequency which inspires the remembrance that you are, in fact, the creator of it all.

The truth is that you can always come home to a greater presence in any given moment. Think about this. If you were actually in a true crisis, say that you just wrecked your car or found out that someone had died, not only would you panic, you would also be needing to handle the next thing. In truth, in the actual moment of a true crisis, one becomes eerily present. It is the gift of shock. Everything slows down, time stops, and that moment is the only moment that matters. You instinctively know what the next thing to do is, whether it is to make a phone call, help others out of the car, and so on. Any moments beyond this are for your choosing.

In current time, you are often wrapped up in a future gaze or past reminiscence and are thus creating from a place that is significantly disempowered, resulting in experiences of fear, lack, longing, or separation. The future is being created with each breath, in each moment. The past is complete. It is done and is ready and waiting to be released. Presence is the gift and the fundamental pause that must first occur for you to get clear and to create what it is that you actually do want to experience.

Think for a moment of all of the things that get to shift when you are in presence. You become more available to listen to your friends, family, loved ones, self, and Spirit. What most humans are really, truly craving and perhaps most in need of is to be heard, received, witnessed, and loved.

When you are not present, you are emotionally, spiritually, and mentally less available to yourself, others, and even God.

When you find presence and eventually master it as your predominant expression, the magic of this world opens up to you in a way that is significant beyond measure. When you are present, you can hear and feel the truth of what IS for you. You can catch the significant communication that the Universe has always been offering you, and it really, truly is significant.

There are messages all around you, in every moment, which so often go completely unnoticed by you. In presence, you hear the directives of your higher self, that soul part of you that holds all of the wisdom of the eons of experiences from this earth-plane reality and every other plane of existence which you have lived through. This includes your past lives, soul memories, truths, and all of the other soul wisdom that has been experienced by you. It is all there waiting for you to pause long enough from your stories of the old pain-body projections of what you don't want but are attaching to anyway. Also waiting are your future worries and woes of all that might go wrong, to show you, with crystal-clear resonance, who you actually are and what is actually and completely possible for you.

Your higher self is the conductor of your orchestra. It is your soul's expression of your most sacred truth. It is in many ways your connection to the infinity of all that is. It is you actualized as the true creator, god/goddess-self. When you are in presence, you have a greater capacity to hear, feel, sense, and know the information your higher soul-self wants for you to remember.

Presence has a profound ability to remind you that you are a multidimensional being who is playing out as a soul expression on planet earth through flesh, blood, bone, sensation, vibration, and emotion. This remembrance helps you to rise above any and all experiences here on the earth plane with the sight of a master, allowing you to see what you could not see when looking through the limited lens of fear, confusion, and chaos.

To find presence, you must first take a pause. The key to getting there is often your breath. When you focus upon your breath, it will bring you home to your magnificent inner workings, to the fresh, potent landscape of infinite remembrance and to the magic of you. Presence creates the pause and gives you the ability to deconstruct the programs of the old, while setting the tone for what it is that you actually are willing to experience.

Presence gives you the ability to catch the next thought or word to make sure it is truly aligned with who you are becoming. Presence also offers you the opportunity to shift frequency and then offer your thoughts or words over with confidence. No, this isn't always easy. It is a practice until it becomes a habit. It anchors in your reality. In time, it will reset your entire operating system and empower you as the master of your own existence.

You have the opportunity to dismiss the chatter of the mind, find the pause, and summon your deepest level of presence. The mind is much like the ego. The more you tell it to go away, the louder it becomes. Instead, thank the mind for all of the wisdom it holds and all of the support it has given you through this human experience. Love the mind into cohesion. I mean, really, it has supported you greatly, but it has also greatly hijacked your soul's voice or screamed incessantly over it at the very least.

Thank the mind and tell it that it has done such a magnificent job that it has earned a break. Then offer it something playful to focus upon. You can't command it away but can rather inspire its greatness to relax, like the queen on her throne. From that place, you usher the soul to step forth and drive the bus for a while, or forever, in time.

The mind is tricky. Just like the two-minute pause you did earlier, the mind will hijack any great moment or intention faster than a dealer shuffling cards in Las Vegas. You didn't get to this place of imbalance between presence, future tripping, and past gazing overnight. Your misbehaving brain has been hijacking your consciousness for a very long time. It has been doing so for a lifetime, actually many lifetimes.

So, you aren't going to deconstruct to reconstruct the exchange and bring it into balance immediately. Be patient, and as with all of it, you get to choose over and over again. Every time you choose consciousness over mind chatter, you are, in fact, beginning to reprogram the mind.

Realizing who is in the driver's seat of your life must occur first. The misbehaving brain has held the throne for so long that you may not even realize the power it has over you. You are being given an opportunity here to realize. Once you see, you can't unsee.

How do you know if you are fully present or if your mind has hijacked your frequency? Well, how do you feel? The indicator is always your feelings which are the expressions of your frequency. When you feel good, you are vibrating high. When you don't feel good, you are vibrating lower. It truly is that simple.

So, if you are dedicating absolute commitment to being present, first you must be able to get clear on how you are feeling. How often when asking someone how they are feeling have you heard "I think I feel…"? You can only be clear about your feelings when you are present and have moved down from the matrix of the mind and into the cellular frequency of your feeling state. This is all an inside game having phenomenal outside effects.

One of the opportunities of presence is that you will have to feel it all. If you have not been present for some time, beginning to feel it all can be quite intense. The pain-body will scream, "Get me outta here!" Many have been programmed in the third dimensional (3D) experience to numb the feeling state. They then often choose to turn off presence through many different vices. There is alcohol, drugs, caffeine, medications, TV or Tell-Your-Vision, games, gossip, constant worrying, feeding drama, overworking, and overexercising, to name a few. However, when presence is summoned, there is an amazing opportunity to feel, to heal, and to rise up.

When you heal the pain and stop the ongoing, crazy mindmatrix of future and past projection, you can then find yourself here in current time. Helloo! In current time, everything is usually okay. Feel that right now. In this now moment, is everything okay? How does okay feel? If you're willing to expand to the next level, you can begin to embrace, from this still point, that truthfully everything is always working out for you. Look back for a moment. Has everything usually worked out for you in the end?

One of the gifts of presence is the incredible communion with everything that exists around you. Let's Play! Go outside, preferably in nature if it is available to you. Set your pulse to presence. Dance with the mind's desire to hijack the given moment by saying aloud, "Thank you, no thank you. I will get to all of that later." Touch your body, touch the earth, touch a tree. Stop, take a breath, take it all in. Close your eyes. Do you feel the sun on your face, the wind in your hair? What do you hear far off in the distance? What do you hear nearby? Can you hear your own breath? What is the first thing that you see when you open your eyes? What is the first thing that you hear? What do you know about these things? Are there messages awaiting you?

This Universe, this planet and all of creation, is here with you, it is here for you, it is one with you. It is speaking to you in every moment. It speaks through signs and symbols, through the whisper of the winds, through the stories of the trees, through colors, numbers, animals, songs, signs, and symbols. There is a holy communion or holy "communication" taking place in every moment, and it is all for you.

In the mastery of presence, you can begin to receive. Receiving is the key to creating everything. There is direction, wisdom, love, and guidance dancing around you always, in every single moment. You are not now nor have you ever been separate from anything. This is your awakening to remember the truth. In the sacred pause and divine presence, you become remembered and begin to seek for proof of connection as opposed to the familiarity of separation. This is the dimensional shift alive within your precious soul right now.

This is a big, bold, messy, and deeply beautiful journey of awakening, of presence, of wholeness, and of connection at its greatest level. It is all alive within you. It always has been. It is simply that now, in this moment, it is more accessible for you to BE than perhaps in any other moment that has ever existed. You are an infinite being living in an infinite Universe of co-creation.

Tirta Empul Temple

During a glorious trip to Bali, Indonesia, I had a brief yet profound experience that forever shifted who I am and how I move through this world. Like many significant markers of time or awakenings, it was subtle. The world didn't shake in the quake of my aha moment. In fact, if I hadn't been willing to be an active and present participant in my life and an eternal student wanting to know with an eagerness to be shown, I may have missed it all together.

In fact, I say this as a reminder that the greatest shifts of consciousness are not always the big rockers of your life's boat. In fact, they are usually quite the opposite. The most profound ahas often come in quiet and subtle expressions, like a leaf falling from the tree or the wind whispering to your heart that is primed to hear at a precise moment. This journey of living, remembering, and becoming is truly profound.

It is approaching the halfway mark during a two week trip to Bali. I have had plenty of time to hand over my western ways and succumb to the slower pace, brighter colors, and full body smiles that the culture so richly provides. I had danced for days, journaled, eaten beautiful foods, enjoyed many spa treatments and sacred sight visits at this point in the journey.

Today we are going to a well-known water temple called Tirta Empul Temple, meaning Holy Spring in Balinese. Since 962 AD, the waters from this temple have been gathered from a beautiful spring sourced from the Pakerisan River. There are at least fifteen cement water spouts pouring these waters forth. Guests are asked to come into the sacred waters fully clothed and in prayer to receive a ritual of purification.

The moment I enter the sacred pool, I feel the warm water melt my sarong to my body, hugging me close like the womb of mother. With my hands in prayer, I turn to the first spout and speak into the waters, "Fear. I hand over the fear that holds me back from living and expressing myself fully." I turn my body and place my head beneath the flowing waters pouring out of the mouth of the cement deity above me. I continue on offering over that which is complete for me as each deity pours its water blessing over me. Spout after spout, I offer over illusion, scarcity, longing, anger, shame, and on and on it goes. Each fountain is like a personal baptism, a release and reclamation. After each offering and bathing in the holy waters, I take a flower from the top of each deity and place it into my own hair.

The lengthy passage to each of the fountains occurs three times. As it all unfolds, time collapses and ceases to trouble me any longer. The presence of purification knows no time. This sacred journey, like most things in Bali, is beautiful, steeped in ceremony, ritual, honor, beauty, and grace. Feeling beautiful and free, I take one final dunk into the massive pool, bow in gratitude, and gently exit the fountain area, high on purification. I am notably expanded and deeply calm.

I, along with my group of fellow retreaters, move to an area behind the pool to change our clothes and wander through the temple. We witness many couples getting married, babies being blessed, as well as what looks like people receiving healings. The ceremonial colors are so profound, and my eyes are dizzy with delight. My senses are at full volume. Every cell is pulsing with presence.

I stand for some time gazing into the most exquisite, purifying waters. The colors of turquoise and blues are like nothing I have ever seen before. I truly feel as if these holy waters had been gathered somewhere else and placed here as a pure gift of love to those who are blessed to enter these sacred and ancient temple gates. In this moment, in my mesmerized state, magic happens.

My dear friend, soul sister, also named Lisa, the person co-leading the retreat, gently takes my hand and asks, "How are you feeling right now?" This question seems to come out of nowhere and sets me back a moment. It's like being jolted awake after falling asleep. I take a long pause, look down at my beautiful batik sarong, touch my heart, close my eyes to find the truth, and as I return to her gaze once again, I finally reply, "I feel nothing."

In that moment, I am filled with everything and nothing. I am fully present yet attached to nothing on the earth plane. I can't feel my clothes still damp on my body. I see all of the colors, the sky, the people. I hear the chatter, yet it has no effect upon me.

I am everything and nothing. It is in this very moment when I realize I am in the zero point, the void. This *is* the zen moment.

It lasts maybe minutes, maybe longer. The next awareness I have is the rain hitting my face. If you've ever been in a Bali rainstorm, you know that they can come out of nowhere and feel briefly like a flash flood. The downpour snaps me back onto the earth-plane reality, and with an outpouring of joy and laughter, we all find ourselves running toward the shelter, and just like that, the experience is complete.

It is complete at least in that moment, and somehow it will live eternal within me. I now know what being free of ego and identity feels like. I've visited the void, the great oneness, the zero point. I know that it also exists right here with you in this very moment, that it is here for you, and that when it is experienced, there is a profound moment of remembrance of the truest connectivity to all things, to Source itself. All the chatter, pain, ego, and even pleasure fall away into perfect union and a profound ease. This is what I consider to be the full culmination of the soul's remembrance, that there is no separation. We are all connected to everything, all of the time.

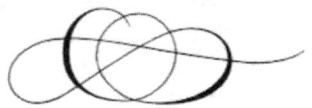

Surrender

"Breathe. Let go. Remind yourself that this very moment is the only one you know you have for sure."

~ Oprah Winfrey

I wake up early in the morning as the sun is beginning to show its first glimmer of light. I find my way down to the cozy couch piled high with down pillows, sheepskins, and fuzzy blankets. Over the years, I have found endless hours of comfort in this spot. I plop down deep into the couch. "I cannot do this anymore," I say to myself, as my body hits the couch like a last breath, an absolute proclamation.

These same words were squeezed through my lips, in this exact spot, some months before, when the lynchpin started pulling from my charmed life, as all was starting to deconstruct. At that time, my beloved was sitting across the room from me sipping his morning coffee, having just found out that our magical home had been put up for sale in the hottest market of the century. As we were mourning the eventual loss of our home, we were sensing that our fifteen-year-old relationship would soon be closing as well.

We were bridging the space between the known and the great unknown, a space determining a change was required, while carrying a part that was so comfortably uncomfortable that fear and confusion were clouding the lens. We were walking into consciously uncoupling a long-term relationship, where love was deeply present, yet a deeper knowing that neither of us were in fact growing prevailed.

We had been sitting in the "I don't know" for many months with the one true thing being known as "I cannot do this, as it is, anymore." It was a beautiful dance between the two polarities until the great clarity, the great knowing, and the clear direction unfolded. It was a dance, a journey of profound curiosity, transparency, vulnerability, and ultimate surrender.

As I sink into the couch, reflecting on the recent past and uttering my true proclamation, the early morning sun crests over the mountain from the east, streaming past the large angel wings hanging in the window, erupting its morning light blindingly into my eyes. I gaze at the sun for a really, really long time. It blazes a golden yellow that literally blinds me from seeing anything else. I do not blink until the light has permeated so deeply that I have no choice other than to close my eyes tightly to it.

Blinded by the light, I begin praying to Spirit, "I cannot take anymore." I feel myself collapsing within myself. "I cannot do this anymore," I say again, this time outloud. "You must lift this burden from me." I feel as if I am metaphorically on my knees. "I am at the breaking point and do not know what it is I am to do." In this moment, I have come to Jesus in all of the ways.

"I have done everything that you have asked of me! I have followed every lead, every thought, every suggestion. I have surrendered. I have trusted and handed it all over. I have voiced my truth and stood in the unknown." Tears are now flowing down my face, soaking through my shirt. I am beyond the point of any control. "You must lift this burden and lighten my load!" I billow. "I show up every day in service. I pray,

I ask, I follow, but I am at the point of breaking, and you must lighten my load!"

I hand it all over at the next level. I literally cannot hold any part of myself up anymore, and so I let it all go. In time, my breath deepens, and I slowly come back to my center. I take another breath, more intentional this time, and a sip of water.

I look up to catch the light of the morning sun, much higher in the sky now, filling every corner of this beautiful room, of this magical home that I have been so honored to live in for the past several years. I am deeply saddened to soon leave it. After several months of intense exploration, I have ten days to move and have no idea where I am going.

Two hours later, everything is shown to me. Where my things and my cat Halo are to go is finally revealed. The arduous journey of consciously uncoupling follows, involving getting our son prepped and ready for college in a new state and the selling of 85% of my personal belongings. All of this upheaval is happening while I am in the middle of reconstructing my online business and as COVID is happening all around me.

Chapter Two
Dismembering to be Remembered

"When the remembering was done, the forgetting could begin."

~ Sara Zarr

As you are creating the New Earth, it is important to remember that you are a consciousness creator, a magic maker. You are the wayshower, the truth teller, the lighthouse. You are the lightworker, and your journey here on this planet is incredibly honored. Thank you for being you on this planet at this profound time.

You are being remembered to the truth of who you are as you are dismembering the old third dimensionality. You are being taken back into the remembrance of who you actually are at soul level. First you must dismember the old illusions, the old limitations, the old scarcity, the old fear-based thinking, being, and creating. You must dis-member to re-member.

Here you are in this portal. The more intentional you are about dismembering to remember yourself into your soul's greatest, most bountiful expression, the more you are committed to that process, the quicker we as the collective get to wake up and move into our greatest universal remembrance. We each get to move dimensionally into our highest expression and really, truly live our best lives. You are here to live your most extraordinary life!

When you are dismembered, separated from your soul-self, you are detached from your truest power and are most likely living in fear. When you are in remembrance, reconnecting yourself into your greatest truth, you are experiencing the full expression of love. There are many lenses to look at this through. The invitation is to stop attaching to and catastrophizing your non-truths.

How do you know that you are operating within your non-truths? You know because you don't feel good. It doesn't feel good when you're in lack or limitation, and you may often find that you're actually fighting to keep that lack or limitation. Do you say that you want something and immediately dismember from your greatest power of creating it into reality? Do you immediately explain why it is not possible? If you choose to fight for your limits, your limitations will then be your reality. The Universe is kind and will give you what you proclaim.

Remember that when you are in the present time, the here-and-now reality, everything is possible. Catastrophizing is future gazing. It holds the energy of anxiety, just as the past gaze holds the frequency of depression. By all means, if you are going to future trip, write an entire story of what will or will not be. Please write a fucking amazing story, not a tragedy. As in all things, *You Choose.*

Do you hear yourself saying any of these statements? *I'm not good at this. It's not my natural state. I know I'm going to fail. I'll try, and we shall see.* There is a stream of limitations available, usually about lack: *There isn't enough. There won't be enough. I am not enough.* When you are experiencing a state of a lack of consciousness, you're in a dismemberment of your authentic soul-self. This is the moment when you will likely begin to fight for it or seek proof for the lack to anchor it even stronger.

We often hear people fighting for their right to stay dismembered, in lack, separation, pain, and suffering. You can hear this externally from others, but can you hear it internally within yourself? *Yes, but! Yes, but you don't know. You don't know how hard I've worked. You don't know how awful it is. You don't know what happened to my family. Yes, but!* Are you fighting for the lack and limitation of the lower third density and your dismembered right to stay in it? Please *STOP* catastrophizing the future you are creating at this very moment!

You begin to remember yourself to your sovereign truth, or others to theirs, by questioning: *Oh, but what if it was possible? What if it did happen? What if there was enough? What would it be like?* The truth is, it is just as easy to stop fighting for limitation and to lay down that sword of suffering as it is to pick up your wand of wonder and creation.

It is in the moment when you come into absolute presence that you become aware of your power to create. You begin to change your mind and remember who you are at soul level. You're an infinite being living in an infinite Universe. You are the creator. Everything's available to you, and it has always been this way. You just weren't able to see it, and the programming that runs so deep holds you in the dismemberment of lack, longing, and suffering of the currently collapsing 3D patterns. You are so wired for it that you want to justify it and attach to the lack. You then want to convince those around you who are not willing to hold you in the limitation anymore.

It is so much easier to see this externally than it is internally, but this is the beauty of co-creation with the Universe. Pay attention to the people you love, to the people who are around you. When you're in your higher frequency and you listen with presence, you can feel the attachment, the distortion, the fighting for limitation. You can feel it, you can hear it, you can be witness to it. You can see it clearly when you are in your most sovereign space of feeling truly sourced. Listen with love to the people around you and hear what it is they are saying.

You often hear and sense dismemberment when people are in fear and future projection. I heard it with a dear friend some time ago. She said, "You know we are in our forties and don't have anything tangible. We don't own a home or have a significant 401k. We don't have enough. We don't! We are going to have to work harder. I have to go do more because I'm going to retire someday, and there isn't enough!" I could feel her pain and her belief in this as truth, can you?

I listened with love and asked, "Is there enough for you right now? As I witness you, it seems that there is more than enough right now." She paused and took it in. Next I asked, "What if there is enough? What if everything is working in your favor and miracles are unfolding for your future which you simply cannot yet see?" I reminded her with love that when we are in a future projection and catastrophizing the outcome, we limit the resources that are available to be plentifully created through us in the here-and-now moment and that every here-and-now moment creates the future.

There is no separation from what's happening today and what you're creating tomorrow or the tomorrows of the tomorrows of the tomorrows that will be. It's all a frequency. What you are attaching to in the here-and-now moment is creating your future reality. When you know this, you are indeed remembering.

The next opportunity for you is to come to a state and space of grace, shifting vibrationally to what is possible, to where you are not just knowing it as a concept but are allowing it as a frequency into your own being. You are no longer fighting for your limitation of what you perceive to be true now but are rather holding a strong expectation of the miracles and magic to come.

Please *STOP* convincing yourself and others that there is something catastrophic to be fearful of in any future creation. The collective of humanity is deeply programmed for this sort of experience because that is how we have lived lifetimes, that is what our families have taught us, and that, my friend, is what will not carry us through to the promised land. This is what we are deconstructing to remember in higher frequencies so that we may all be free, so that we may all be the divine creators that we actually are, no matter what proof we have in the here-and-now moment of any limitation.

You can absolutely prove in most situations the lack. My questions are then intended to prove otherwise: *What if there was enough or even more than enough? What if tomorrow everything changed? And, what if your remembrance allowed for you to be sourced in a sovereign way that holds no attachment to the limitation of the old life you have experienced because you are now ushering in a New Earth in this very moment?*

It is up to you in every moment, with every thought, every word, every belief that you hold. *What are you willing to remember? What are you willing to attach to? Are you willing to hand it over and stop fighting for the limitation, no matter how real or how true you perceive it to be? How committed are you to the attachment to your pain-body and the fear in the lack? Are you willing to be free and create like a master universal baller in unity with divine creation?* You choose.

The entire world is on the brink of a massive transformation. Your inner world, your outer world, they're both a perfect breathing organism of NEW. The sooner you remember the truth of your soul's wisdom and release the programs of the mind that are holding you in the limitation of the dismemberment of your truth, the sooner you are willing, the sooner we shall rise together, the sooner we shall usher in this New Earth, the sooner we shall all be set free, and the sooner we can get to living as we are intended to live, as a true member, in a true remembrance and membership, membering together as one.

The rise of new frequency is here. It is here. It is here for you now. These words have been spoken so many times and for so long in consciousness communities. This is the magic sauce, my friend. You have a greater capacity with this fifth dimensional (5D) frequency to attach to your vibration, your understanding, your crystal-clear understanding. These are not just words. It is a resonance of how it feels, and once you feel it, once you're attached to it, once you "remember" to it, there is no going back because it feels too good to be remembered in the truth of it as such.

Be present. *How are you creating your future? What are you fighting for? Are you fighting for your limitations? Are you fighting with your fears? Are you fighting for the mechanism of the mind or the expanse of your soul?* Because the new frequency is here. It is here for you. It is here for each and every one of us.

We are at the brink of no return. We are expanding rapidly in consciousness, and this is swooping through humanity. The collective has reached a capacity of understanding that is nearing the tipping point. Every thought we have ushers us closer to that tipping point, to the point of no return. This is the point of not going back to the lack and limitation of what we had once been living. This is the point of bringing in utopia, yes utopia, of true soul expression of living, being, having, breathing, realizing that it is indeed all here for us, the bounty that has actually always been here for us.

This is not to say to throw all planning for your future to the wind. Be wise. Be conscious in your choices and creations. Do so, however, without fear and with a grand expectation that all is going to be better than imagined, with a true knowing in your bones that everything is always working out for you, that the Universe is kind and gracious and deeply longing to create and provide miraculously through you, and that everything you desire is indeed possible to be experienced by you. EVERYTHING! Change your pulse, open wide with trust, appreciate with gratitude, and watch the miracles unfold right in front of you.

A few months later, my aforementioned friend went on to experience a living, breathing miracle. The home that she and her family had been renting for many years was offered to her for purchase in a way that made it both possible and truly miraculous. She then went on to purchase fifteen acres of pristine land in a very exclusive part of the world where we were both blessed to live.

It is all frequency, and the frequency shift is a pivot of your proclamation in every breathing moment. You have been dismembered from the truth of your soul's greatest expression for long enough. You are now becoming remembered as the divine creator that you have actually always been. Bring light to the shadows and rise in your remembrance.

You are a magnificent warrior of light. You are doing such an amazing job of awakening to remember on planet earth at this time. I know this is not always easy, but it shall be worth it. You are not alone. You are greatly loved. You are powerful beyond measure.

The Deer

The smell of wildflowers is hanging lightly in the air, the sun is dancing through the green of the fresh new leaves presenting themselves proudly on the trees above, and the emerald of the hills is almost blinding me with wild delight. I am high on the bliss of this very busy, well-traveled, beautifully winding road that runs about eight miles from my mountain abode to the beach town of Carmel-by-the-Sea, California.

I am late, as I often am. Time is one of those constructs of the 3D reality that has never seemed to completely fit my natural expression. I am driving too fast, playing with the stretching of time rather than choosing to be anxious and resistant to the clock.

I round what is perhaps the deadliest corner along the entire road. A few sacred souls have given over their life on this stretch of pavement, and I can definitely feel it as a sensitive person. As I lean into the curve, there she is, a beautiful deer lying half on and half off the side of the road. Her head is held up high above the road, but her body is not moving. Beside her is a man in a big white truck who had rounded the corner just a few minutes before me and had obviously hit her. She looks up as I approach, and we lock eyes.

I can feel her stun and panic. "Am I okay?" she asks me with her gaze at this precise moment. I know instantly that I am there to help her and that somehow she is helping me in exchange.

What I am struck with most, beyond the distraught, kind-hearted man who is already on his phone summoning some sort of help, is the wonder of who should be called in a situation like this. I am also mesmerized by the depth of connection I feel to her. I know she is a female and can sense that she is pregnant. I feel all of her move through me in a flash, all of her. I feel her with such connectivity that I know we are switching over into the next realm of pure soul communication.

I feel one with her. I feel her fear, her shock, and her pain. I move into prayer and say to her through my heart, "I am here with you. You're not alone. I hold you in hope, honor, and love. I thank you for sharing your scariest moment with me."

I pull over half a mile down the road, tears now streaming down my face. "I give you permission to trust that you are safe and are free to go," I continue with the prayer in my heart. This level of communion with her takes me by surprise, more so than the shock of rounding the corner to the scene itself. I weep out loud, a sobbing cry of what feels like the primordial pain one feels when a soul is rocked and loss has occurred.

I have no idea if she made it or not. I am holding the vision that she is simply shocked and will get up in time and run off to continue her life's journey. By the time I return a few hours later, there are no markers that anything had ever occurred.

In that moment of the medicine of the deer, she reminded me to be gentle and to trust. Things are not always within our control, and we don't always see what is coming just around the next bend. The message is to care deeply for self, to pause in each moment for presence and gratitude, and to trust even when it feels as if the bottom has fallen out or when life has just swooped in for a massive change in an unforeseeable way.

I am so grateful to her precious soul and have decided to see her as free, running through the meadows with her babies in tow. I have received her message, as I hope you do as well, to be gentle and discerning and to take such good care of self that all other care flows naturally from your full, highly supported, overflowing vessel.

This is the power of presence. No, it's not always comfortable, but you are here for it all, in co-creation, at a level that your mind has no capacity to understand. We know at soul level that we are deeply connected, becoming more and more so daily, as we ascend through to the higher dimensional realms. In our presence, we can then commune with everything and take it all in. We begin to see ourselves as an expression of every living thing and separate from nothing.

Yes, there is pain to be processed at this level of connection, and more importantly, there is love, grace, and goodness to be explored as well. The Universe is always communicating with you. There are messages in every single thing that is shown to you. You know you have landed at the next level of presence when you begin to know this and begin to receive and exchange in every moment with everything that is. You have an incredible impact on everything. Everything that exists is responding to you as you are to it.

This level of awareness is exactly the place in fifth dimensional clarity that is unfolding for humanity, not just to understand but to experience, embody, and become. Each and every human is waking up to remember that he or she is a supersonic conduit of pure frequency, separate from nothing, having effect upon everything.

LIGHT COUNCIL CHANNEL

"We come forth this day to set order to what you perceive as chaos. There is a divine flow, a sacred union, perfect harmony, and a time for all things. We want each of you to know that your greatest gift is your BEing. Even when you perceive that all is awry, even then, especially then, in your sweetest surrender, there is divine order and an opportunity at hand to BE: to breathe, to allow, to sink into the divine splendor of your human living, to go with the flow.

The sacred rivers of consciousness will always lead you home to the promised land of your sweet soul and your precious heart. It is not now, nor has it ever been in the attachment to things, or people, or a place, or a way of being that your greatest expression will be found. It is in fact in the subtleties of your breath as it touches the wind and carries your divine essence far beyond you on high into the expression of all that is.

You do not yet know your power, for the ability to see it was taken from you some time ago. Worry not. It is and will be regifted through you, and when you wake up to your fullest power, to your fullest light frequency, in that very second, all will settle, all will be revealed to you and through you. You are the creator. You are the wind, the light, the entire circumference of all beings.

The key, dearest one, to getting you there? Your love! It is not the love of the limited mind but rather the love of your infinite soul expression. The pure love of your authentic and true frequency is your road home. We are here on high offering direction, a clear path for you to find your way home to this truth. You are the most magnificent creator of reality that has ever been. Take pause as you receive this remembrance and allow these words to penetrate deeply within you.

The moment you strip yourself free of the illusion of separation is the moment grace will occur. You will then take a deeper breath and will once again know. Once you are fully remembered, you will never again forget, and in that moment, you will rise to such a grand place among all things that all of those in your presence will rise too."

- The Light Council

Pillar Two
CONNECTION

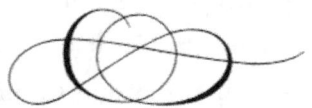

Trust:
Surrendering to Spirit

I sit here gazing across the great expanse of far sweeping views. I am in awe and silence, knowing that all great things come to pass, that all great ideas are created, lived, and in time find their finale. All beauty fades or perhaps transmutes to express itself in new ways. For everything there is indeed a cycle, a season, a death, and a rebirth.

I take a deep breath, reveling in the silence that I finally have found after weeks of emotion, fear, and so much fucking work. The silence is broken only by the caws of the crows, a hummingbird diving past my nose, the wind blowing over me, and the occasional sound of a car finding its way up the mountain from the village far below.

The color of magic fills the air, as the sun shoots its glorious rays across the valley's expanse. This million dollar view I will never forget. The smells of summer sage, dry grass, and wet earth touch not just my senses but also my soul. In the silence, beyond the days and the weeks of exhaustion it took to deconstruct everything, I can finally let the tears flow.

This home, this life is complete. It has been so for some time.

I watch the sun as it sets in the nearby Pacific Ocean. I express my gratitudes and pray for peace. "What a journey," I think as I get up and walk through the completely empty, now spotless house with the golden amber light pouring through it, the sacred light that holds the frequency of the space in between. It is the same light that the sun offers as it rises to meet the new day and summons one to rest at the end of it. There is a moment when the difference is imperceivable.

I close the door for the last time and walk onward, down the street, wondering where I will find my next Palace of Light. Before I know it, just a few days later, my best friend and consciously uncoupling partner is dropping me at the airport in San Francisco. I'm off to Maui for two months so I can heal and write. As the plane lands, I realize that I have just done the hardest thing I have ever had to do, or at least that is what it seems like at the time.

Chapter Three
Who is the Light Council?

"We cultivate love when we allow our most vulnerable and powerful selves to be deeply seen and known, and when we honor the spiritual connection that grows from that offering with trust, respect, kindness and affection."

~ Brené Brown

There are many councils of light beings making contact with the earth plane at this time. There is the Federation of Light, the Council of Light, and numerous others that are too many to count. The Light Council has explained to me that these are all expressions of similar energies coming from on high to support the collective of humanity through the process of awakening.

They are benevolent beings, star beings, other-dimensional beings, angels, guides, and ascended masters, all operating from different planes of existence. For many, many years, people have been channeling these light beings, but now, more than ever, a great number of them are coming through to offer guidance, clarity, and an opportunity for massive acceleration and ascension.

The reason for the grand increase is twofold. First, we as a collective have raised our frequency so rapidly that it is now easier for us as humans to connect with light beings. As our frequency rises, it is also easier for them to connect with us.

Many here on planet earth are also of starseed nature. A starseed is a being who holds DNA remembrance of off-planet existence in one or more of the star systems. This resonance or remembrance connects one to his or her galactic family.

The councils connect to support the collective of humanity through the awakening portal and the shift from third dimensionality, through fourth density, to the fifth-dimensional frequency. The councils are here now because they are our allies to support the massive awakening of planet earth.

The light beings need us to awaken as much as we need to awaken. They explain it like this: *"It is for you to remember that any pain or poor cell growth in your physical body over time begins to have an effect upon the whole body. You may have a small skin abnormality as you would perceive to be a "cancer," and that small growth is fine for a bit of time. It may even be there for many years unnoticed, having little impact upon the whole. It also could begin to grow and begin to affect the other healthier cells around it. If left unchecked, it could begin to destroy the entirety of the well cells, and life or function as you once knew it would be marred. This is true for planet earth as well. There are malevolent beings who have held you, planet earth, and all of humanity in a depressed state for many thousands of years. There were agreements made about this many "years," as you perceive them, ago. It has come to a point where the density has gotten so "dark" that it is indeed having an effect across the galaxies. We the councils are here to support the evolution and the rebirth of your planet and of all those who inhabit it so that the collective of all may stay intact and in turn rise up to the next levels. You are not here to suffer. You are pure light, and it is in your remembrance that you shall not only be set free but shall rise up to an extraordinary frequency of harmony that you cannot yet even begin to imagine! We are honored to be here with you."*

It is crucial that the councils of light beings make contact at this precise time to bring through our remembrance. They support us to elevate in frequency and navigate this wild and amazing dimensional shift we are currently riding through. They need us to rise and remember for the galactic good. We need them to help us rise and remember to wake up and move out of the destructive, dense, fear-based way we have been existing on planet earth for far too long.

Gaia, our earth, also needs us to wake up and to live in harmony with one another and with her. She has suffered greatly in our dismembered treatment of ourselves, each other, and this amazing planet we are so blessed to inhabit. Gaia herself has spoken through me. She said to fear not for her ability to regenerate goes far beyond anything we can comprehend. She has indeed seen it all, more than we will ever know. Our history has not done her story justice, as we are so limited with the lens of which we can currently see, and we have been shown very little of what is true.

All of nature regenerates. Every cell of your body is completely transformed and becomes new every seven years. You, nature, earth are all biomechanisms of continual regeneration. When we remember this fully, we will stop aging and suffering and will ultimately have the capacity to expand our lifespans exponentially. This is yet another thing we will awaken to remember.

The programs of the mind run deep, so deep. They are deep enough to make you forget how magical and powerful you are as a divine presence. They are powerful enough to let you think that you are limited in any way. When you operate from that perceived limitation to create a reality of it, you are not able to see that you are the one in fact creating it.

How to Connect with Light Beings

Everyone has the capacity to make contact, receive information, and channel. Just as every human on the planet is a medium, a psychic, and an intuitive, everyone is also a spirit channel. The connection to all experiences and expressions is part of the expansion into higher consciousness, bringing you to know that you are in fact separate from nothing and connected to everything.

The beauty of this time in which we are living is that the consciousness of humanity is vibrating much, much higher. Your own vibration is vibrating much higher. It does not take years but rather weeks, days, or even minutes to begin to channel or to truly allow the shared exchange of energy to emerge through you. The illusion of separation is blurring its lines, and the act of channeling is more and more becoming an extension of your higher thoughts and higher self. In time, we will simply call it sharing the source of absolute wisdom.

How do you know who you are connecting with? It is best to always ask, and the being will tell you. It is also important to ask if the being is here for your highest good. If you aren't getting a clear directive as to who it is that is communicating through you, you can ask a friend to ask questions, the first one being, "Who are you?" As you allow more and more channeling to move through you, you will find that different beings hold very unique frequency patterns. For example, the Pleiadians come in with a very fast frequency. It is a very buzzy, high-pitched energy for me. They speak fast and are very excited to make contact. Over the years, I have come to identify the different collectives by their vibration, and they, in time, clearly tell me who they are.

Proceed Consciously

Not all beings that knock on the door are always of the highest light. It is essential to be very discerning. Set up a filtration system in the beginning of any channeling practice with Archangel Michael, the Protector, whose name means "He who is like God." Ask him to ensure that only those who are here for the highest good may enter into your energy field. Each time a new frequency appears, the first question is always, "Are you here for my highest good?" By universal law, if they are not, they will then go. It is important to remember that you are of free will and you are in charge. You choose. You decide yes or no. It is also of high service to ask each being to leave your own being in a way or a state better than they had originally found it.

It is also noteworthy to say that the experience of channeling beings is an edge for many. Remember the Lady in Red? I had to move through a lot of fear about being judged, shamed, persecuted, and abandoned by society or by my family and friends, yet here I am now in my fullest expression. It is a calling, and when you are called to your highest level of service, there is an opportunity to rise to new heights, heal the fear and trauma of old, and fearlessly forage forth.

Let us remember as well that many have had past-life experiences on planet earth where they were persecuted or even executed for being the seers, the wayshowers, the bridges between worlds, and even the witches. This is the lifetime where those old persecutions shall be made complete.

Atlantis was the last lifetime during which humanity existed in celebration of our greatest gifts and powers. In many ways, our awakening is aligning us back to the remembrance of that time, as we are fully sourced and expressed as soul beings in human form. As we collapse the 3D limited lens and awaken to remember, we are realigning to these gifts and allowing them to become our greatest service.

We are now discovering greater connection to self, Source, Gaia, and to each other. How you get there is by being present, listening deeply, forgiving the lifetimes of torment, trusting that you are safe, and allowing for your vessel of consciousness to open for greater receiving and ultimately offering. It is safe to be you here and now in your greatest expression. There has been no greater time for you. Shine on you crazy, beautiful diamond, and allow these benevolent energies from on high to show you, to show us through you, the way home. Heaven on earth is awaiting.

Chapter Four
Dimension Shifting

"Energy can never be created or destroyed, only changed in form."

- Albert Einstein

Everything is frequency. Dimensions are frequencies, not physical spaces or a physical reality. They hold a significant effect upon all of the expressions of you: physically, mentally, emotionally, and definitely spiritually. The awakening process you are riding through is a shift in dimensional frequency that is happening in every expression of you and of planet earth.

Dimensions are levels of consciousness or the vibrational frequency at each level that you and the collective at large are vibrating within. The third dimension is the dimension you are most familiar with. It is the frequency that you and the collective consciousness at large have been vibrating within for several thousand years.

The third dimension holds a frequency of separation, of longing, and it is far too often held within the pain-body as a tool for growth. This frequency vibrates through every expression of you. It is expressed through your thoughts, feelings, words, and your entire life's experience. It is so familiar that to shift frequencies into a higher realm literally feels like hard work.

The current rise in consciousness is the portal of awakening we are all walking through at this time. This great awakening is the opportunity at hand to rise up to a new frequency, how you get there is through a process of remembrance and the intention of this book. Although the shift feels as if it is a challenge, what we are doing is rising up to remember the truth of who we actually are at soul level. Living in the lower third dimension has been the challenge, yet it is also the opportunity for profound growth. To live in a shadow of one's soul truth actually takes a greater amount of energy than that which is required to remember and to rise. This is the good news.

The fifth dimension is a frequency that vibrates at a significantly higher resonance and has a perceived faster pace as a result. This is why time has felt so distorted. Time in fact is changing. The frequency of 5D, in its faster flow, leaves you feeling as if time is slipping away. How many days do you wake up, do a few things, and look at the clock only to realize that most of the day has moved rapidly through you, like the blink of an eye?

The beauty of this higher dimension is that you will begin to feel connected to all things from this place. The illusion of the 3D separation gives way to a remembrance that you, from a soul level, are in fact one with everything. You are one with everything you have ever longed for: money, things, people, experiences, states of being, everything that vibrates on planet earth, which in turn is everything. Remember everything is frequency.

From the 5D expression and the release of separation, you become one with the truth that you are a master creator. If there is to be no more longing and no more separation, manifestation then becomes an effortless expression or extension of you. It has always been available to you, but the deeply woven programs of the 3D mind have held you locked and loaded in the illusion of separation and longing. You have been living in fear and lack from that lens. The lack of consciousness has you believing that everything is outside of you and that someday, if you work hard enough to prove that you are worth it, you will then, maybe then, have the things you desire and find your truest joy.

Every longing or desire you have experienced from your 3D living lens actually exists because the thing of desire is already vibrating within your energy field. You would not have a desire if it was not already alive with you in some frequency. Herein lies the illusion of the 3D lens. You think you want something because you believe you will be better for the experience of having it and because that thing of your desire is so close and has come into your awareness. From this old lens, we often feel the thing, and then the old programs enter right on cue to tell you that you can't have it. The sensations come through via negative questioning and thinking: *Who do you think you are? That is too big! I am not yet ready. This is for them, but not for me!*

The 5D experience will, in time, have you remembering that you are, in fact, a master creator. You will understand that you are worthy because you exist, that whatever you desire is here with you as soon as you align with it and become one with it. This new frequency allows you to KNOW that it is in fact here with you, that this has been why you have desired it. From the higher perspective, the second the thing of desire is recognized, it is in fact revealed. You become an instant grandmaster flash creator! Actually, you have always been. You are now releasing the programs of the old density to remember, and the moment that you do, everything changes. It is Creation Game On!

Why would we ever choose to live in a 3D world?

It is important to understand a bit about the galactic history of planet earth. Several thousand years ago, there was a battle that took place over the governing of the free will of humanity. There were dark, malevolent forces at play who battled for power over the earth plane. Similar battles continue and are what you have been witnessing playing out on the earth plane for many, many lifetimes. Part of how this has operated within you as a human is that you have been coerced into forgetting that you are the gods and goddesses of infinite creation. The process has been slow, arduous, and long. The mind is subtle.

Over many millennia, programs have also been interfering with your greatest remembrance. In modern day society, these programs have increased in a phenomenal way through TV or Tell-Your-Vision, media, and now the countless social programs that exist. These programs run so deep, through so many generations, through so many lifetimes and have gotten to such an extreme point that fear is used as the predominant force in keeping you asleep. The more asleep you are, the easier it is to coerce you to hand over your free will and your remembered truths and powers.

If you look at how society has progressed over the past 150 years, you can clearly see a mass increase of pharmaceuticals, chemically created foods, massive global toxicity, additives in water and food, TV, social programming, and on and on. So much is at play to keep you in a somber state of lack, both disconnected and unconscious. This puts you on the hamster wheel as you work harder and harder for less and less, increasing the longing for something outside of you to make it easier.

The Light Council revealed that the forward progression of humanity was at odds several decades ago. This planet and the life upon it had moved so intently into the depths of third density that we, as humanity, had to decide basically to rise up or to stay in the density and risk destroying ourselves and the planet. We collectively chose to rise. Here we are now, in a time like no other in the history of planet earth, making a collective soul decision to ascend, to remember, to rise, and to be free from energies manipulating your freewill.

With the support and influence of our galactic friends, we have been on a journey of ushering in the higher frequency. It has been said that every human on the planet at this time has made a soul agreement to be here to usher in the New Earth. This means that each of us must release the lack, fear, pain, separation, and limitation of the old and allow ourselves to be remembered to the truth. We are to rise up. It is in our rising that the powers of old will be and are being dismantled, bringing us back to a sovereign consciousness.

The 5D reality is utopic in many ways. It is also just a stair step to even higher frequencies and dimensional experiences. Not an end goal, but a step upward to higher and higher dimensionality. This time has been prophesied for thousands of years. It is written about in the Bible. We are indeed living in end times, but not in an apocalyptic, armageddon, everything-will-be-destroyed sort of way, but rather that everything that is holding humanity in the old frequency will be dismantled and destroyed. This will occur so that earth and all of its inhabitants will awaken to a time of great love and unity. You will be living as a fully expressed soul with love and light as your guides. Sounds too good to be true? Believe it. There is a part of your soul's truth whispering through these words that remembers, that knows, and that said "Yes!" before entering the earth plane. Your physical vessel is to be here now, and you are here to actually usher it all in.

You are worthy because you exist! The benevolent beings on high often tell me that we, as souls living in human form, are the talk of the galaxies. It is one of the greatest honors ever to be witnessed to be a human during these extraordinary times. All souls who have chosen to be here have done so with soul agreements to lift themselves up to their greatest expression and greatest power in love and light, to usher the light through into its strongest frequency, and to lay the dark to rest.

In the fullness of 5D or greater, you will be fully remembered and forever free. Each choice you make, each thought you think, each word you share will be in alignment with this higher frequency, and the entire collective of humanity will rise together in time. Each soul holds a different mission or agreement within this dimensional rise. Some souls are here to birth the new energies as part of their mission, others are supporting the emergence by becoming light bodies and leaving the earth plane. This is why we are currently witnessing so many precious souls departing at this time.

Can you imagine a time when money has shifted away from the painful illusion of the debted society we have become so accustomed to living within? When people will see all living things as an extension or expression of self? When humans will work in unison with Gaia in service to her, just as she so graciously serves us? When every living human has everything that is needed and more? When humans do what they are best at and love most as a contribution to the collective? This is the New Earth! This is the fifth dimensional frequency. Welcome Home!

What about the fourth dimension, the often forgotten yet very important stepping stone? It is best to think of the third and fifth dimensions as stairs and the fourth density as the riser between the two. The fourth density is the bridge, if you will. It would literally blow our circuits to shift dimensions in one fell swoop. The shadows of awakening come if the leap happens too rapidly or without the space and support needed for integration. Many have "lost their minds" as we perceive it. Collapsing one state of being and moving into another is a precious, delicate dance. The fourth density gives each of us the needed space to integrate and adjust. You can think of this space as the neutral bridge between two destinations or experiences.

As you are awakening, you are moving between all three expressions: 3D, 4D, and 5D. Few on planet earth are living fully in 5D, at least during this time, as these words are being written. Many are walking up and down the stairs. It is truly like being on a rollercoaster or a Ferris wheel. Being in 5D feels so, so good! I like to say that many are now experiencing the pleasure of reaching to the sky of the 5D expression. We are feeling our way through. Many are finding their grace and waking up in the fourth density, licking the sky of the fifth, and then tumbling back down to the oh-so-familiar 3D.

Each time you come back down, it is actually more and more uncomfortable. Remember, you are remembering, literally bringing the pieces back together, reMEMBERING your higher self to your actualized human living. The more you journey to lick the sky, the more pieces of your fully sourced, sovereign-self come back to the forefront, the more you release the programs and the patterning of the old. The higher up you go, the deeper down you plummet, at least for now. You must come back down to gather, heal, and bring the lost, fragmented parts of yourself home. On and on the journey goes, and you will eventually spend more time in the higher frequency and less and less in the lower.

Although this journey sounds euphoric and profound, and indeed it is, there are also some hurdles along the way to overcome. The journey can feel incredibly isolating and sometimes lonely. Not all souls are rising in the same frequency or in the same time frame. All will rise or leave the earth plane in time, but the journey to getting there is intense and arduous. As The Light Council has been saying through me for years, "The journey is not easy, but we promise you it shall be worth it."

Much must dismantle as one dimension deconstructs and the other builds anew. This plays out through every expression of you. You will feel differently, think differently, talk differently, choose differently because you are vibrating differently! Everything you created through the 3D lens will be up for review. This has an effect upon your relationships, job, home, community, hobbies, and so on. In truth, there will be no stone left unturned along the way.

All must rise or release. The polarity of contrast and the density within each expression will define each next step taken. I am witnessing and experiencing some of the things created in the old literally becoming intolerable, while other things feel fine to hum along into the great unknown, at least for a period of time. Remember, this is a deeply personal journey with a mass collective effect.

To walk this path with others, it is essential to find those with similar consciousness, frequency, and desire to awaken. Remember the 3D is separation and scarcity, the 5D is unification, co-creation, and harmony. You do not need to go this alone. Reach in to your truth and reach out to attract those of a similar truth, even if you don't yet know how we shall rise together as one in commUNITY.

Here I will give you the most clearly defined expression I can share to identify the difference between 3D and 5D. When you are operating in 3D energy, you are locked in the expression of the mind. You are thinking your way through, trying (a great 3D word) or working hard (another great 3D word) to understand it all, to figure it out. To operate in 5D energy, my friend, you must figure "in" and not out. The answers that lie withIN you, as the intuitive, sourced, sovereign being that you are, come from your soul's truth.

The mind holds the programs and limitations that keep you locked in the old. (I believe the mind works through the operating system of the brain and expresses through vibration.) Imagine the brain as a master computer or even as your smartphone. It requires updates every so often to bring it up to speed. At times, it also needs to have old data or programs removed and old systems extracted. Then there are viruses that pollute or disrupt its capacity to run clearly and smoothly.

Your systems are constantly in need of purging the old and upgrading the new. Your mind is no different. Your mind has been programmed since day one of your entry onto the earth plane. No matter when you believe that moment occurred, while in utero or upon your first breath, you have been programmed, as were your parents, and those who came before them.

It would make sense, like any master computer, that your brain, i.e., mind and conscious or subconscious expressions would need to extract the old and bring in the new from time to time.

When you are in the higher frequency of 5D expression, you are in your feeling state. You have moved out of the matrix of the mind and into the soulular expression of feeling. You access this state by moving down the sequence of your inner workings from mind to heart, to solar plexus, to gut or the womb room as I like to call it.

**To access the Womb Room Process,
please scan this QR code.**

The 3D frequency thinks, while the 5D feels. How often do you ask someone how they are feeling and they reply with "I think, I feel…"? From the feeling state, you have access to the rapid expansion of 5D reality, a state you will never ever arrive at via the mind. Your higher self communicates through the cells of your body. This communion is part of the quantum experience of being a human being. You have the capacity to feel your soul's truth through the resonance and frequency of your human body. How insanely amazing are you?! We are here as humanity bringing heaven to earth, and it all starts with you switching your predominant operating system from your thinking mind to your feeling BEing. You are a divine soul living in an expression of bone, blood, and flesh.

Have you ever had truth chills, or truth goosebumps, when something or someone resonates with you? This was the first thing that became alive for me as I was waking up as a seer, a healer. When my intuition was fully online, I would find a resonance with truth, whether receiving information in my innersight or from the external plane, and my body would chill. Your cells resonate when truth and connection to divinity is present. You know! You feel it! You ALLways Know!

In every moment, the opportunity for you is to choose whether you are going to think or feel your way to the next expression. In every moment, you are choosing. In time, with consistent choosing to be present in all ways, to feel your way through, you will expand more and more into the 5D expression, and the programs of the mind will eventually fall away. You will eventually see clearly the truth beyond the veils of the great illusion. You will see with your real eyes and realize who you actually are. Once you see, you can never unsee the truth, and in that moment, you will begin, with every breath, to move more and more fully into your fullest 5D or higher, heaven-to-earth, soul-in-body expression. As you rise, the entirety of humanity will rise, too. The old collapses, and the new arises, like the dawn of a brand new day.

The fun truly begins with the clear understanding that the end game is by no means reaching the 5D expression. In many ways, that is just the beginning. The journey between collapsing the 3D density and rising into a lighter 5D expression and experience is exactly that, a journey, an arduous journey. Once you and the collective of humanity rises to this next frequency, the rise upward to higher-dimensional experiences will seem like a cakewalk in comparison. This IS the most challenging of all leaps. Once we are settled in the higher-dimensional frequency, the journey of expanding to the sixth, seventh, eighth, ninth, and dimensions beyond will be a much easier ride.

It's like getting yourself out of quicksand in the middle of a storm. You may still have a journey to find your ultimate destination, but once free from the strangulation hold of this level of separation, the rest will be much more like a walk instead of an arduous climb. So much more awaits than you or I can begin to imagine from this point forward. Exciting indeed.

The Bali Spider Story

I first wipe the sweat from my hand before I can get ink to the paper. My body is still buzzing from the ecstatic dance jam I had just lost myself in. I pause to look out over the rice fields that are so beautiful in a way quite unfamiliar to me. The Bali landscape is wet and humid, the sun is blazing, and I am in wonder to find myself here. There is a feeling of absolute presence rushing over me as I close my eyes to reflect upon the wisdom my body has just shared with me.

I take a moment to gaze around the open-air temple, admiring each of the beautiful souls from around the world who are gathering with me. I release the powerful energy that has just moved through me as my breath begins to calm. I find my center once again. I settle into my body's truth and retrieve another realization of the old, stagnant ancestral energy that is wanting to move through my pelvic floor. As it does, it creates a significant amount of pain as it shifts.

With another deep breath, I begin to journal, unfolding my body's truth word by word. In the next minute, I feel her, a blurry flash of brown furry light moving at a supersonic speed. I feel the pressure upon my pubic bone first before ever seeing the yellow glow of her eyes. "AHHHHHH," I shriek, as all eyes turn to me with just enough time to also catch a glimpse of her. She is easy to spot as she is larger than the palm of my hand.

Grandma spider had come seemingly out of nowhere, running across a large expanse of floor to find me, leaping right between my legs, landing upon my yoni (lady parts), and scurrying with absolute fury straight up the front of my body. She ran straight up, touching each of my chakras in a split second. When she crossed my heart, she paused for a brief second. I swear she looked into my eyes just as she scurried over my face and then leapt off my third eye, landing upon my crown. There was not even a second to integrate when she jumped onto my right shoulder, sliding down my right arm, off my fingertips, and across the open floor for all to see. She then jumped over the floor's edge and was gone just like that.

After grandmother spider vanished, I burst into tears, fully receiving her deep medicine working through me. It was as if she performed her own cellular massive clearing and activation on me in that moment. It was profound, palpable, and truly exhilarating. The pain in my hips began to subside over the next several hours, as my ancestral trauma shifted in some undefinable yet profound way. She, grandmother spider, took a piece of what was complete with her, leaving me in awe and somehow lighter, healed, and profoundly grateful.

The spider brings in the wisdom of the ancients. Her medicine is stern yet loving, like a grandmother. She is the great initiator of the feminine mystery to be remembered. She brings the shadows to the light to be seen and awakened. Her web carries your dreams on high to the light of the dawn, allowing them to be made manifest. Her bite is potent and her power is strong. She carries the wisdom of the ancestors within her womb. She is the wayshower, the storyteller, the wisdom holder.

Everything in, of, and around you is a gift. The entire Universe is working with you and through you. Everything is here in co-creation with you; it is in your presence and your willingness to be a co-creator that the magic and mystery begins to reveal. The Universe is always here supporting and serving you in all of the ways. You simply must move into greater presence to be able to see, feel, hear, and know all of what is being offered to you and through you, as you are shifting through these dimensions..

The Universe speaks in signs, symbols, numbers, shapes, colors, and codes. She speaks through the plants and the animals, through the stones and the clouds. She is here speaking to you, showing you the way home. It is for you to discover what each of the markers mean. This is the communion, the co-creation of oneness, that is here supporting you through this life's journey upon this amazing earth.

Chapter Five

How 5D Plays Out on the Earth Plane

"Progress is impossible without change, and those who cannot change their minds cannot change anything."

~ George Bernard Shaw

I truly believe I had been stair-stepping through the portal of awakening over the entirety of my life. One of my first spiritual awakenings took place when I was quite young, already living on my own for a few years. One night, I had a truly magical experience with two girlfriends. I had known them both for some time, and they were just becoming acquainted. Together the three of us experienced a time leap, and I think the catalyst for this was the watching of the movie *Dances with Wolves*. I'm honestly not sure what exactly it was within the movie that led to our wondrous experience. Nevertheless, it was a night like no other.

For three young women who are stone-cold sober, time leaps over a several hour period. As I lay back from the circle we've been talking in all night, I begin to watch the journey of my life through my closed eyes in the theta space, the state between dreaming and being awake. As I am transported through time and space, almost like watching a movie, lifetimes unfold. I am eventually cascaded back to sleep, and when I wake in the morning, a calling is alive within my belly.

I am living during the time of Operation Desert Storm, and I am just twenty years old. I have just leapt through several rings of my spiritual journey overnight, in a flash. Soon after, I am summoned by the earth herself, by Mama Gaia. She is calling me to commune with her. I am terrified yet excited about what I am being shown. Her message is clear. I am to sit with the earth each day. And I do. I sit on the earth for hours on end. I am also to give my menstrual blood to the earth to balance the spilling of blood through death, war, and suffering. She calls me, she summons me, she asks for me, with all the love in her heart, to exchange my energy with her so that we can both heal. I am both confused and deeply grateful to head the call.

For your free downloadable Gaia Activation Meditation, please scan this QR code.

The collective of humanity accelerated its move through the initiation gateway during the Winter Solstice of 2012 on December 21st. This is when the initiation of the New Earth's entry began to ascend into our collective consciousness. If you remember, this was said to be the end of the Mayan calendar, known as the portal of the great awakening. I must say, as a spirit channel and a spiritual teacher, I was really naive about the big picture of how this would all play out here on the earth plane. I thought, with great delight and a dreamer's heart, that we would awaken, ascend, and transform, that rainbows, butterflies, and all that is magical would be here with us.

I've always been able to sense where we were going but had a very limited understanding of everything we would need to do, deny, deconstruct, and become to get there. I never thought about what this all actually meant in our earthdance and living expression until the day came when it all became crystal clear, when my "reality" collided with a higher knowing. Things started revealing themselves rapidly, and the great uncloaking of illusion was upon me. Can you relate?

Then entered the great COVID pandemic of 2020, when we, the humans on planet earth, began to awaken to the truth, to how this was really going to play out through our reality on the earth plane.

The year 2020 was a four year, numerologically speaking. The number four destroys old realities and recreates new, stronger foundations and structures which everything is to be built upon in a NEW way. It was during 2020 when I began to realize that if there was, in fact, a massive awakening happening, and if we were to release everything that was constructed in the limitation of the old 3D lens, well then, "Holy Shitballs, Batman!," that meant that all of our modern-day society structures must shift, too.

Money

When I look at the foundational core of the deconstruction of the 3D lens as it plays out on the earth plane, I am brought to one of the greatest energy expressions of our time: Money!

Every foundational structure we are living within has been created and based around money and a for-profit society, with all of its institutions, structures, and expressions. This includes government, healthcare, education, justice systems, prison systems, and on and on. If we are to create a New Earth, then it must mean that we need to pull this thread of for-profit systems through the matrix and create something new. Does the financial system need to collapse to create a 5D reality of service to the whole as opposed to service to itself? It feels as if the answer is a resounding YES!

Money is a construct of human creation. Humans created it much like time. Money was created to mark an exchange of energy. It actually is energy. We created it, empowered it, came to fear it, blamed it, and used it until it shifted the ownership of power and started using us. Remember the shadow of the 3D lens has been locked in longing, lack, loss, and separation for a very long time. This definitely plays throughout the energy of money.

Money is simply an illusion made of paper. It was once backed by a tangible asset, such as gold or silver. At one point, it then moved into a system of digits and paper backed by nothing, hence the illusion. It is far too often used to control and limit the masses while serving the few. Then when debt was created, our sovereignty was willingly handed over.

I was on a call with a longtime client shortly after the pandemic broke out. Her concern was heard in her inquiry: "What if it all collapses?" She was genuinely worried about what would happen if the financial system fell apart. The current system has been based on money as the source of our wellbeing and security. There is also an innate feeling within most, if they dig deeply, that this system of survival is not sustainable. We know from a logical mind and a sovereign feeling that this money creation must shift if we are to rise up free from the slavery and oppression of it as it is currently being played out.

How much money is on planet earth? An infinite supply! Studies have been done through calculations to reveal that there is enough currency on the planet for each human to have hundreds of thousands of dollars. In reality, there is more than enough for everyone. And, yet, simultaneously, it's only real because we as a collective society have attached an energy of value to it as we devalue ourselves in the face of it. Go figure. You are an infinite being living in an infinite Universe, and this is the truth. There is actually enough for everyone, and then there is more, a whole lot more!

Unfortunately, when we moved into becoming a debted society, we moved out of sovereignty and into a deepening well of lack, longing, and suffering. Our systems are set up for profit, leaving behind the sovereign soul's truest desire for wellness and thriving for all. In fact, it has been shown through The Light Council that there are many technologies existing here on planet earth right now which could support free and endless energy, cures for many common diseases, and infinite possibilities to lift us up and out of this pain matrix. Sadly, however, they have been kept from us because there is no profit in bringing these systems forward. There is no profit in your well, whole, vital, and fully expressed self, not within the "old" paradigm.

The sad truth of modern day living is that money is made upon you staying sick, working hard to survive, and chasing the tail of money itself. It is an endless journey of doing to survive, which is in direct opposition to your BEing to thrive. The Light Council once said, "It is time that you all make your peace and get right with money, for in the moment that you do, money as you know it will shift, and everything within the foundations will rise to a new currency."

My aforementioned client was scared at the thought of losing the abundance she had attached her security and wellbeing to. While we were speaking, I was shown a huge wall, stacked high to the heavens, and just over the crest of it, I could see a shimmer of light. They showed me the wall being torn down, brick by brick. As it collapsed, the brightest light I have ever seen began to stream from behind. They said, "Fear not for the new has already been created."

The light is here. Just behind the illusions and the veils of limitation, awaiting the crumbling of the old, the light of the new is here to emerge freely forth. This light will reset the old 3D limitations and make way for the rise of the quantum currency of the new, where everyone has everything that they need provided for them, where people are served to be well, no longer sick. Systems will be constructed to create freedom and ease, where every human on planet earth will be cared for so that we may collectively rise up and shine in our light. It is all here waiting for us to rise up as one. We must say "No more!" to the old and "Yes!" to the new. We shall then all rise up and thrive in well-being. This is indeed our birthright!

There was a time in humanity when the healers were held as the most revered in all the land. They were paid well for their services for it was understood that the miracle of healing was an exchange of energy. Those who could see, feel, intuit, and offer healing were honored above the surgeons who needed to cut through flesh to cure. We are awakening to this time again. When the collective is fully remembered and the technology that already exists is made available, the entire healthcare structure will shift.

There was also a time when doctors were paid to keep you well. They only got paid when you were healthy. If you were sick, they were not doing their job and would then tend to you to bring you back to wellness. Wow, how things have changed. In this 3D lens, they are paid to keep you sick and keep generating pills and services through you to keep profits high. You clearly see and have lived where this structure takes humanity.

The opportunity is now here for the collective to say "No more!" and to stop playing this game of unwell, broke, and sick. It is time to rise to the truest light of infinite potential, to shift the matrix, even the playing field, for the good of humanity. You are witnessing this play out at this moment. You might wonder what your role is within this? It is to wake up, see the truth, make decisions in your daily life which stop feeding the engine of the old, and start leaning into the possibilities of the new. This is what your soul agreed to and is how it is playing out on the earth plane at this time.

Guess what else collapses in 5D?

Karma

As we dimension shift, another aspect of transformation is karma. Karma, as I see it, is a 3D construct. The basis of karma is that you are born forgetting everything, must then fully surrender into complete care in the entry stages, and are here to live the lessons of what your soul missed, or even correct some karma that was created in the previous round. You go about growing and getting imprinted again during the present journey with the souls you chose to be born through, your family.

It is also noteworthy that the entire purpose of choosing your parents, from a soul perspective and from the 3D lens, was based on who your soul felt would give you the greatest opportunity to expand, fulfill soul contracts with, and ultimately, yup, you guessed it, play out karma with. It is not the universal soul agreement that the parents you chose were to give you the greatest love or even the best leg up to live your greatest life, but rather you chose them based on if they would set you in motion to fulfill your karma.

From that lens, each and every one of them has done a magnificent job. So, whose job is it to fill you up with love and light? Yours! It is your job to fill your well, and you do this with each choice you make, such as what thoughts you think, beliefs you attach to, people you associate with, and the way you choose to feel.

If the karma game is an opportunity to learn, grow, and expand, it also serves to create through that experience more karma. It's an endless loop. You learn, grow, fulfill contracts and lessons, usually through pain, and then in the process, you create a few more deficits for the next journey around to come in unconscious, learn again, grow some more, heal some things, expand in some ways, and fuck up a few other things along the way. On and on the journey goes! WOW, sounds like a fun kaleidoscope of expansion and contraction, doesn't it?

It has been an exhausting journey for thousands of years. It makes sense that if this new frequency of higher reality and consciousness is upon us, and the old pain-body limitations are falling away, then karma itself must change, too.

You are an infinite being living in an infinite Universe. From this lens, you expand by remembering the truth of your fully expressed self. You will no longer learn through contrast and pain. In the old frequency, you would learn what you did not want to create by what you did create. This is called creation through contrast. You had to walk through the land of shadows, karmic creation, and contrast to expand.

As a fully sourced being, sovereign and remembered, you create through pleasure, frequency, and alignment. Remember that from the 5D expression you are one with everything. You would no sooner hurt your brother or sister than hurt your own being because you feel it all, you feel everything at an extraordinary level. Karma completes as the old 3D cycle falls away.

This also brings you to the realization that the life, death, rebirth cycle must shift as well. Every cell of your gorgeous body regenerates itself every seven years. Does it make sense that your cells age, weaken, decline, and fall apart, that you die after seventy to one hundred years? Maybe not.

What if it was all part of the limiting program from the 3D lens? Would it make more sense to stay here remembered and thriving for hundreds of years? If heaven is coming to earth to live as an advanced soul-self, and karma is no longer the game, then why go through this old, limiting process of continually starting over?

With the technology that exists here, being made more and more available to you, and the inevitable entry of higher, more advanced systems, and the complete ascension in consciousness, it is possible that the experience of aging and death will also need to shift in time.

Do you see how deep this rabbit hole goes into the infinite possibilities of what awaits you, as the old falls away and the new light emerges? The possibilities truly are endless, as is the capacity for your soul and your cells to rejuvenate. The journey of becoming New Humans is upon you, and the Universe and beyond holds no limits.

When do we get there?

I was once asked, "When do we arrive in 5D? Will it ever get easier? Will it always be this hard?" I have to say that this journey of dimension shifting is not child's play, nor is it for the faint of heart. Each of our souls agreed to this journey, and we collectively are here for it all, or we leave the earth plane.

As I am writing these words, I have to say in full transparency that I am watching the wobbling and shifting of 3D creations first hand. Talk about finding comfort in the discomfort, finding trust in the unknown, finding the sweet or not-so-sweet surrender. Everything is up for review. As we deconstruct the old, one thing is indeed crystal clear, everything must rise or release.

The answer is that you are already there. In so many ways you have welcomed in the New Earth. You are licking the sky of the fifth dimension and are mostly anchored in fourth density at this time. It is almost as if you are watching a live broadcast. There is always a short delay from broadcast to viewer. We are in this great flux, and it has already occurred in a multitude of ways. Your consciousness is simply catching up to the reality of it as we play it out on the earth plane.

When you are feeling that the goalposts keep moving, The Light Council says you must remember that this is an evolution of consciousness. You are evolving along with the entire collective of humanity. This is occurring in a way that has never occurred before. It may feel as if you have arrived, and then you blink your eyes, and there is, in fact, another aspect of the journey to turrese. It is not so much that the goalpost moves but rather you have a clearer vision of the next opportunity at hand as you rise in consciousness. Let us remember that dimension shifting isn't arriving at a place but rather at a frequency. Each step along the journey is, in fact, arriving, and then there is the next step to the next rise in frequency, and on and on it goes, and on and on we grow.

Some in the consciousness community believe that as humanity arrives at the precipice of the new, there will in fact be an event, a great event, a light blast, that will occur in one flash, and we will all awaken from the illusion-filled slumber, and kaboom! we'll be awakened. They've even set many dates for the grand event that have come and gone. I, however, perceive this shift to be more of a sequence of events, an experience of transformations, where we are stepping up a ladder of ascension, walking a path of initiating into a completely new expression.

There are no goalposts. You have arrived at every moment as you feel resonance to a higher frequency. You arrive again, and again, and again until that frequency becomes anchored in, and then there is the expanded next-level frequency.

Will it get easier? Yes, it will get easier the moment you choose to surrender. In time, it will get lighter and lighter for the collective as well.

As you are ascending through the dimensions, you are most likely experiencing these moments of everything being in alignment. It feels amazing, maybe even ecstatic. There is ease, then you dip back down into the third dimensionality, and each time you dip down, it feels less and less comfortable. The dip occurs for you to learn from contrast, as that is one of the laws of attraction of the old, contrast to grow. *I don't want that any longer, so I must then want this.* You also dip down to gather the pieces and parts of yourself that are fragmented or have fallen away in the 3D matrix. You are resurrecting the pieces and the parts of self. This journey requires humans to collectively bring themselves back online to remember who they are from pure soul expression. It feels like we're working so hard. Let's remember that working hard is part of the third dimension.

We are looking through the two lenses of 3D and 5D. It is hard to focus clearly through both lenses at the same time. Imagine that you are looking through binoculars. One eye is looking at 3D, the other is looking at 5D. Both eyes are trying to get the focus sorted so that they are pointing in the same direction with clear vision, so that you can see well enough to realize what's actually happening. There's an adjustment, right? You have to adjust, and if you're working hard to adjust, it is an indicator that you're holding that resonance of the 3D lens out of focus.

What we're doing is deconstructing an experience that has kept us from our greatest truth, our greatest souls' resonance. What we're deconstructing is the hard dense part, and where we are going is toward ease. The "no pain, no gain" expression of the old is not gonna bring us home. The Light Council says that when you choose to be in the frequency of ease along the pathway of becoming new humans, ease shall meet you there and carry you home. You get to choose surrender over and over again, and the sooner you do, the sooner all of the powers of the Universe swoop in to carry you to the next greater expression.

When we get back into that trusting space of surrender, we trust the Universe, and when we are not too far in the future and not too far in the past, we move into presence. We are back into our power of presence and our trust that the Universe is kind. We are aware that we are awakened live souls here to usher in a new way, a remembered frequency. The best is yet to come in so many ways in our expression as souls here on planet earth. We must choose trust and must keep rising up to that next level of trust over, and over, and over again, surrendering over that which is done, complete, limiting, tiring, and fear creating, until it is done.

It is in the moment that you surrender, in the moment that you choose, in the moment that you trust, when all of the Universe's intelligence and wisdom comes to life within you and shows you your way home. Breathe that in.

In some ways, we have to let go of everything we have ever believed and have ever intended in order to rise up to see what is here for us in this new way, in this new light. We have to trust to the level that we have never been called to trust before. It is here. It is now. We are in it.

We are in the active birth of this New Earth in this here-and-now moment. It is like, for those of you who have birthed children, when you want to push and you're told, "Wait! Wait and breathe. Don't push just yet!" During this moment, there is so much discomfort in the waiting to push, and you just want to move to the next level. It is in that moment when you take a deep breath, go a bit deeper, expand a whole lot more, as you wait just another second. That is where we are. It's crazy, it's wild, and here you are.

I am often asked when this will all end. We will be there when the tipping point occurs, when we have all risen together. The tipping point of activating the consciousness of humanity into a higher frequency occurs when a critical mass of consciousness has risen past a certain point and reaches critical mass. That tipping point, that 100th monkey syndrome (described below), is when something is recognized by enough consciousness that it becomes the collective consciousness.

A group of scientists were once researching monkeys on an island in Japan in the 1950s. The monkeys loved sweet potatoes but hated the sand they would find them in. One day, a monkey was seen washing a sweet potato in the river. As the scientists continued to observe, they began to see that more and more monkeys were washing their prized sweet potatoes in the waters. This in itself was not phenomenal given that as "monkeys see, monkeys do."

What was fascinating was that monkeys, in a short manner of time, were observed on all parts of the island washing their sweet treats. Let's say, to keep with the storyline, that 99 monkeys were doing this ritual over time. One day, the 100th monkey joined in, and then voilà, this is when the phenomenon occurred. Very shortly thereafter, scientists on several other islands began to witness monkeys washing their sweet potatoes in the rivers before eating them. The scientists believed that there was a tipping point in consciousness.

When enough minds connect with one thought, that thought then becomes a collective knowing. When enough of us rise into the same frequency, all rise into the same frequency, which ultimately births the New Earth. When this occurs, we will be anchored in the frequency at the highest level. This requires patience. It requires perseverance. Nevertheless, our souls have agreed to this. We were made for this.

The great-grandmother is a 5D being. She is sitting in the corner, rocking in the rocking chair, watching the room. She is calm, patient, curious, taking it all in. There is a smile on her face and peace in her soul. She has nowhere to go for she has arrived. She is in pure splendor and awe of where she finds herself, holding such great wisdom for all she has seen, experienced, and come to know. She is pure presence, great ease, and absolute contentment.

On the floor in front of her sits the three-year-old child. The little one is having a fanciful time scurrying about the floor, pulling out toys, moving from one great thing to the next. She plays with one toy, then with several, starts another game, then another until there is a bounty of joy splayed out everywhere. She then becomes upset because she cannot find something she wants and begins rolling around in a temper tantrum. Up she goes again seeing the kitten, happy again, then over there to the next thing she goes. The child is the mind finding its way, uncertain and overstimulated, young in many ways. The great-grandmother is the soul with all the wisdom gathered through many lifetimes experienced in different dimensional frequencies. Both are existing within the same space, yet are having very different experiences. Yes, the child can come and sit on the great-grandmother's lap and enjoy the ease of the moment, but does she stay there very long?

Are you sitting, rocking in the chair, with the soul wisdom of the elder, knowing all will be well because the wisdom and patience is there? Or, are you scrambling around on the floor having fun and then not, up and down, round and round, wanting it now, not seeing that it already is here with you? What expression are you choosing? In every moment, you get to choose the frequency which you are going to attach to. Is that easy? It is not always easy, but each time you choose, it does indeed get easier.

The Light Council has been telling me for years, "This journey is not always easy, but we promise you it shall be worth it."

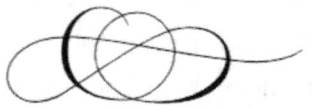

Hawaii

I arrive on Maui midday to meet my dear friend and her precious son, a child I was privileged to help birth onto this earth with open arms and heart. As soon as I see them, they place a lei around my neck. The smell of salt, plumeria, and tuberose takes over my senses and eases me out of my beyond-exhausted, hypnotic state, a state I had found myself unable to shake for nearly two months.

My hopes are high for this magical Maui adventure. As I arrive at my friend's house just outside of Pā'ia, I am shocked at how much this once quaint town has changed over the decade and a half since I had last been here.

I decide to give myself a few days to rest after the arduous journey I have just been on. Every muscle is sore. I have lost weight. I am literally black and blue from all of the sorting, lifting, selling, packing, and moving that had just occurred, as I deconstructed my entire life and my 3,300 sq. ft. home, not to mention my bruised heart. I rest.

The days fly by, and I can't seem to find my steady ground. Each day, I wake up before the sun rises in awe of the magic, the splendor, and the beauty that is all around me. The view is stunning. There is nothing between me and the ocean other than the Hana Highway.

Each day, about an hour after the sun rises, the winds begin to howl, and I mean HOWL. They are relentless, howling from sunup to sundown. They are so loud that I can't hear my own thoughts, and they are matching my internal swirl. Some days, I dance with the winds. Other days, I open up my computer to write and stare at the blank screen. I ask Spirit to guide me, heal me, tell me, show me something, anything. "Please Spirit, show me the way," I pray. I receive crickets.

The only time I truly feel good is when I am adventuring to one of the amazing beaches or waterfalls, gathering with friends for a swim with the turtles, hiking in Olinda, or savoring a nice meal. I also enjoy finding my way to the local yoga studio to get my daily fix with a beautiful yoga teacher named Samantha. I can write nothing, and each day a repetitive message is delivered in one way or another: "This is a journey of death and rebirth."

This message of death and rebirth continuously comes through. At one point, Spirit tells me, "When you are fearless in the face of death, then and only then will you be eternally free." I understand this as describing all of the fear burdening people as they navigate the pandemic and how powerful fear is in moving people to hand over their sovereignty. FearLESS and powerFULL then becomes my motto. I begin to understand that presence is the key to everything and that each and every breath is a death of that moment and the birth of the next. I begin to see in my presence the cycle of everything. I can't seem to write, but I am definitely being molded like clay.

I attempt to put the pieces of my business back together. After decades of entrepreneurialism, workaholism, overdoing-ism, overgiving-ism, and every other "ism" you can add to the mix, I cannot seem to pick up the stick. The only time I truly feel good is when I am simply BEing.

I wake before the sun one day with curiosity as to what my next steps will be. I am struck with a powerful realization that I am indeed getting the chance to embody so many of the teachings that have been pouring through me during the past many years.

As I witness the illusions of the 3D matrix beginning to crumble collectively, it is mirrored only by the crumbling matrix of my own sense of self, identity, purpose, and expression. I am being forced, or gifted really, with the profound opportunity to begin the process of deconstructing my own belief systems, my own 3D attachments. I am feeling forced to sit down and be, while the resistance in my head and my heart is so big. The clamoring is so loud. I am witnessing the death of parts of my own self, my old self, the one deeply programmed to action, the one who never stopped doing. The me who overgave, overshared, overworked, overproduced, overgenerated, and overindulged is now dying.

The wildest part of it all is that in this deconstruction phase of self everything is actually alright. I have everything I need. There is enough money, time, space, love, joy, and laughter. When I let the space BE okay, I am okay, too.

Tim and I text or talk most days while I am gone, especially in the first month. We are still navigating our shared financial lives and our son. The truth is we love each other deeply.

We are completely in awe and shock of who we are being and who we are becoming. Who would have ever known that we could be this conscious in our love to actually let go to see what was possible?

Just days before the big move, sitting in our bedroom, I asked, "You are getting excited about this change, aren't you?" He looked up at me a little startled. "It's okay. All I want is for you to be happy." We both took deep breaths. "And for me to be, too," I added.

He relaxed a bit, looked me in the eye and said, "I think I might be. It's time that I figure myself out." We went on to discuss how things could get challenging living in a small, intimate community and even wondered what might happen with us in time. We agreed to always be kind and loving towards each other and to always stay open and curious as to what is possible.

As the weeks move on for me in Maui, I realize that I am in soul deconstruction, a death and rebirth cycle; there is no picking up where I had left off. I am so uncomfortable most days. There is no business as usual. There is no way to finish this book at that time. I must let go. Most days that is hard, so I learn to let it be, and from there, a piece of my soul begins to transform.

I am called one day to book my return flight home. I buy my return ticket back to California with four weeks still remaining in my sweet Maui Palace of Light. There is one day and one day only that seems to work for a return flight the third week of the month. I am so confused by this, yet I go ahead and book it, figuring I can change it later as the departure date gets closer. My mind asks, "Why would I book a ticket to leave Maui seven days earlier than expected?" In time, I understand the power of divine timing and the Universe's perfect plan.

A good friend visits during my last week on Maui. The plan is that we will fly back to the mainland together. Ah, we have so much fun swimming, mermaiding, playing with turtles, marveling at the sunrises, cleansing beneath waterfalls, hiking, shopping, all the things. I excitedly say, "Let's Stay Longer! We have this house for another week." So we get out our computers and pull up Hawaii Air, and voilà, she can seemingly change her ticket for free with no problem. This is exciting, except mine is not allowing a change.

So we call the airlines. After several attempts back and forth, neither of us is actually able to get any dates to change. My wise friend, also an intuitive life coach, looks at me and says, "It's not meant to be." I look up at her, our big brown eyes meeting in a moment of pause and clarity, and say, "You're right. For whatever reason, these original dates are when we are to go."

As I sit in the plane during takeoff, all I can ask myself is, "What's next?" I was hoping to come home with a finished manuscript in hand, a reconstructed business, and a clear vision of my next step. I am returning early instead with no more than a single page added to what I thought was a nearly finished book. Even so, I am grateful for a sunkissed, yoga-filled body, a quieter heart, and a greater expanse for BEing. I am satiated, mystified, and still wondering why the Universe brought me here to paradise to rest for seven weeks.

Chapter Six
The Ferris Wheel of Awakening

"Life has its ups and downs. When you are up, enjoy the scenery. When you are down, touch the soul of your being and feel the beauty."

~ Debasish Mridha

As you move through this journey, there is one thing that is an absolute: What goes up will most likely come down! There is a massive shift of awakening for the consciousness of an entire collective of humanity; it is personal on the micro and collective on the macro. What you can expect is to rise up to a very high frequency, often feeling amazing. You may also find yourself in extreme lows that are incredibly uncomfortable. Make no mistake, the spiral down is a very important part of the journey. You need both spiraling up and down to ascend.

It seems true in my own experience, as well as witnessing and supporting many through this journey, that the come down is in equal proportion to the rise up. Let me explain why.

You already understand the principles of dimension shifting. This is not a place but a massive frequency shift. As you move to each floor, you will experience the bliss of having landed in the new frequency, and it takes time to anchor it all in. It would be nice to take one big leap and land firmly in the new. In truth, however, the full acceleration into the higher realm all in one fell swoop would destabilize you so rapidly, as it has with some. Such a rapid leap, in fact, would be quite challenging to adapt to and manage in everyday life.

So you lick the sky of the higher dimensionality, shifting incrementally, and then find yourself dipping back down to what is and has been familiar for over thirteen thousand years. It is exactly like a Ferris wheel. Each turn to the heightened space brings you a greater opportunity for anchoring in and becoming more of the new, and each dip back down gives you an opportunity to see with your newly adjusted lens just what is truly happening here in the 3D world.

You must see it all clearly to awaken. You must see beyond the illusions and how you have been an active anchor of the lower density in order to choose another way, forgive the old, and make the choices and changes necessary to rise up again.

Each time you rise, you have left more of the density of the old behind and anchored another piece of the higher 5D consciousness into your cellular and soulular memory banks. It is very much like stair stepping. You step up, see clearly, lose your footing, step back down, regroup, step up again, and perhaps this time you anchor on that step a little stronger and a bit longer. In time, you are fully on the next step and no longer feel a need to step back to the old. It is a cycle of wash, rinse, and repeat because the next step up is always awaiting you.

Sounds exhausting, doesn't it? And in many ways it is. Spirit's guidance has told me for many years, "This journey of awakening is not easy, but we promise you it shall be worth it." Up and down you go, growing with each new rise. It is very much like children taking their first steps. They are wobbly as they first begin and become more sure, steady, and confident in time. Before you know it, they are walking and then start to run. Again they fall, but this too becomes strengthened in time, both natural and effortless.

Just like you, you are learning to walk in a new way, with new legs, and a different gravity, and you will eventually be running free in your fullest 5D expression. What is important is that you do not stop ascending. Do not give up. You get up again and again until you anchor in your energy. When this happens, you are also anchoring in the energy of the collective to step up and rise up to new heights and greater expressions. Together we rise as one.

The beauty of the Ferris wheel image is that it carries you. You got on the ride. You agreed to it as a soul before your earth-plane entry. You got on the ride at that moment. Your soul knew exactly what it was saying "Yes!" to. In fact, your soul was so brilliant that it knew, and still knows, that this moment in time, here on planet earth, is one of the most extraordinary moments in all of human and planetary existence.

Your soul already knows what the full 5D frequency experience is, what it looks like, how to do it. It understands the miracle that is awaiting you and all of humanity on the other side. Your soul is brilliant. It is your mind that is playing catch up.

The souls on planet earth at this time are the celebration of all of the galaxies. YOU are the celebration of all of the galaxies. You truly must know how extraordinary you are on the earth plane, extraordinary beyond measure. Celebrate, especially when the Ferris wheel dips down. You are integrating the next level, simply and beautifully, to rise up again.

In time, you will exit the ride at the highest level, fully awakened, fully remembered, and in the fullest expression of the New Earth. At that time, you will begin to live as a fully expressed soul in a sovereign, fully supported world, a world that is free. This journey of awakening is not easy, but it shall be worth it.

LIGHT COUNCIL CHANNEL

You are but a small speck in the collective gasm of all of infinite creation, yet you are significant beyond measure. Do not tarry in the ways of loss, of confusion, or of unknowing, but move instead toward the flame which is burning brightly inside of you still.

Whether it is a flicker or a full blaze, know that your wisdom, your innate knowing, and your capacity to live within the realms of a life that is unfathomable in its grandness and its greatness is available to be procured by you in any moment of which you are in the choosing of it.

Do not become sideswiped by illusions of things such as failures and insignificance. Focus instead upon the flicker or the flame that is alive within you. Grow it. Fuel it. Expand it. Allow it to burn away the cobwebs of insignificance, of lack, of loss, of frustration. As that flame burns brighter, so shall it burn away all of the obstructions to the truth of your eminent expression, and so shall you move into the fullness of your light.

There is no place of which you are needing to go. You are to seek only for the knowledge that is alive within you. As you spark each cell of this innate knowledge, you shall be transformed. You will know peace. You will know laughter. You will know the soaring heights of what is possible for you.

There is nothing of which you are to seek for at this moment. It is in the allowance, in the letting go, in the purity of trust, and in the connection to the infinity of light that is all around you, that you shall find the sovereignty of which you seek. You shall be the sovereignty of which you are.

You are the radiance of infinite wisdom, of infinite possibility, of infinite eternal light. The magnificence of your soul breathes anew on this day the cycle of your birth, the initiation of your light cycle. You are coming into grace and fruition, into presence and purpose, into power and pause. This day is significant in each and every way. Embrace it. Allow it. Become it. And shine.

- The Light Council

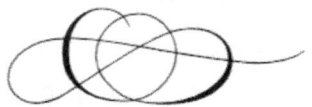

Crawling Home to Carmel Valley

It is well past midnight, and the curving mountain road is the only thing between me and my bed. It has been a very long and exhaustive day of travel. Each bend of the road climbs higher and higher, finally hitting the summit at one thousand, two hundred feet. The lights of the Salinas Valley on one side give way to the fog rolling off the ocean on the other. The late summer heat has the hills a much dryer, richer golden blond than when I had left them just seven weeks before. Ah, I breathe in the smell of home rolling through the cracked windows. I first notice the chill. My body is not accustomed to the late night seachill rolling inland, even in this very late August. I walk up the stairs to my sweet guesthouse, familiar to me only five days before I basically dumped my belongings inside and flew away. I swing the door open and hull my multiple bags through the door. Halo, my cat, looks up at me with shock and awe. Not sure what to do, his eyes open wide. "Hi baby," I whisper to my precious purr purr. He rolls on his back and gives me his belly. I am sure he was as shocked to see me as I was to land "home" in this sweet place I had no connection to, other than with my Halo and the things I had managed to unpack before my vanishing act.

I am exhausted and wired, wired and tired. I finally fall into sweet sleep just before 3:00 a.m. and spend the next day adjusting and acclimating to "home." I am jet-lagged, and my head is spinning. I am realizing I haven't yet dealt with the completion of my relationship or my old life in any way. Landing home has everything rushing towards me.

The next day, I go to town to get some groceries. I swing by Tim's work to say hello. It's a quick hello since he's working. We share a few laughs, I show him my new tattoo, and we make plans for breakfast the following morning. "Let's get clear," I say, "on how we are doing this uncoupling thing." He laughs. I realize in this moment that he has been very clearly living our separation for nearly two months. I was the one just getting started.

We also confirm a dinner plan for Sunday night to take our son out for his nineteenth birthday and to get all of our plans made for delivering him to college in Oregon in a few short weeks. I say goodbye and drive away. I am feeling happy to be back and yet still within a spin regarding what being home actually means now.

Pillar Three
DECONSTRUCTION

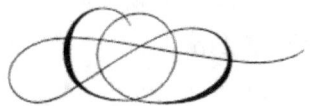

The Night that Changed Everything

"Last night I lost the world and gained the universe."

~ **C. JoyBell C.**

Teresa, my really good friend and astrologer, did a reading for me a few years ago. She said, "Lisa, your life isn't going to look anything like it does today in a year from now." This lit up a piece of my soul. My mind started playing with the possibilities of my future reality where I had published my first book, bought the house, lost the twenty extra pounds, and my business had finally done all the things that had been predicted it would for a few decades. I was living my best life in my forward hologram self. I had no idea the level of deconstruction I would need to go through as her vision of my Saturn return would unfold before me. I had no idea about the death to rebirth cycle I was going to have to walk to finally rise up anew.

I have been home for less than forty-eight hours. I can't sleep. It is a warm night for California but feels cold to my skin, blood, and bone, now conditioned to Hawaii. The moon is pouring its waning moonlight through the skylight, lighting up my mini Palace of Light. I am restless, uncomfortable really, a sensation I feel as if I am beginning to get used to. "When will I feel settled again?" I ask the whisper of my heart. "When will I feel as if I am home? What is home now in this new energy I am riding anyway?" I'm alone for the first time in fifteen years, yet I know, somehow, that it is all temporary.

So many questions, no real answers. It is almost 12:30 a.m., and I crawl into bed. Just then my phone rings. I see it's my brother-in-law Joe who has never called me, even once. "Hello, Joe?" I answer. "Hey Lisa," he says in his thick Long Island accent. "It's Tim," he continues. "He's been taken by ambulance to the hospital. It might be his heart. We aren't sure." He continues only to be interrupted by my sister-in-law who steals the phone from him. (Tim had miraculously ended up moving across the street from his sister and her husband when we consciously uncoupled just seven weeks before.) "I talked to him as they were putting him into the ambulance," she says, "he was sorry to wake us." We kinda chuckle at that as it is so like Tim! "Okay, I'll meet you at the hospital," I say, getting out of bed to go. "No, we can't go into the hospital," she says, "because of COVID!"

The hospital tells her to wait ninety minutes and to call them back, given that he's just being brought in and there's nothing they can tell us yet. "Maybe this is the health wake-up call he needs," I say, and we agree to keep each other updated. I call our son to let him know and tell him not to worry, assuring him I'll be in touch as soon as I know anything.

I lie across my bed, half in the covers and half out. My cat curls up around me. The moon is pouring in through one of the four skylights above, bathing me in a perfect puddle of moonlight. I feel timeless, neither old nor young, neither human nor angel really. I am drifting between the realms as I lie washed in the milk of the moon. I find myself playing in the very illusive space between being asleep and awake. I suddenly remember to set an alarm to call the hospital back at 2:00

a.m. After I set it, I allow myself to merge with the moon. My breath slows as I drift gently asleep, my eyes no longer able to stay open.

I am startled by my phone ringing under me. What feels like hours is just minutes. I reach through the covers and answer the phone. "He didn't make it!" I hear Maya wail on the other end of the line. "What?! Maya WHAT?! No MAYA no! What do you mean MAYYYAA?" I cry out. I cannot breathe! I ask ten more times what she means. This cannot be happening! "Omg, I have to tell our SON!" I shout as I hang up the phone.

I immediately call my just-like-family friends. First I call Plasha, and six times I reach her voicemail. Then I call Randy another four times until he picks up. "Tim is dead," I manage to push out of my mouth now that the full shock of it has enveloped me. "I need you to take me to Satchel. I can't drive." My body is fully shaking now as I try to walk across the floor to put on clothes. The only thing I can find is a sweatshirt with "Grateful, Thankful, Blessed" across the chest. Halo starts meowing loudly and scratching at the door to get out, clearing sensing me in a state he has never before seen.

Randy arrives in ten minutes, and off we go. I am being driven in the middle of the night to meet my stepson and his birth mother. I rush into the house, hold her and Satchel's hands as I tell "our" son that his fifty-year-old father has just died unexpectedly from a blood clot that created an aortic dissection which tore from his abdomen to his heart.

What unfolds over the next hours, days, months takes me through the portal of the initiation of death that one only knows after having been trampled by the beast herself, dragged around through the mist, thrown about, tossed in the air, and landed hard for what feels like a thousand times.

Grief is a bitch of a beast, a fierce dragon, who will have her way with you on her terms, in her way, in her time. She picks you up and takes you in the middle of the night. You haven't slept, you haven't packed, your not dressed, you're not prepared, and she does not give a royal fuck. "Now you are mine!" she screams.

Death is a right of passage, an initiation that most of humanity will be drug through at some point. It is potent medicine for those who are blessed to live long enough to lose so deeply. Death teaches you about life. Death teaches you that each breath is precious. Each exhale is a death of sorts, and each inhalation is a rebirth. In fifty-two years of living, I had never walked the death-grief spiral of initiation, and when she showed up at my door, she was by no means walking me in gently.

Chapter Seven
Letting Go

"Sometimes surrender means giving up trying to understand and becoming comfortable with not knowing."

~ Eckhart Tolle

There comes a moment along the path of this journey, a point of no return, where everything begins to change. It begins subtly, as most significant things do. You notice that you're not loving your routine in quite the same way, a few of your friendships are feeling exhausting, work may cease to satisfy as once it did, your lifestyle and habits come up for review, you don't want to do the same things in the same way or even with the same people any longer.

As the journey of awakening moves along its course, there comes a time when the inventory has been taken, you are clear about what you'd like to rise or release, or at least you think you are, and then the matrix begins to tilt, the lens shifts, and your reality begins to crumble, or at least that is what it feels like. No stone will be left unturned. The deconstruction phase comes through you and comes for you, as everything in this reality does.

Your greatest fear will undoubtedly arise, the thing or expression you have put the most attachment to. You then meet the demons of deconstruction, and everything begins to change. It has to. It can feel like a complete reorganization or a complete annihilation. This may even be experienced as "the dark night of the soul," and many will need to journey through these depths to rise up, resurrected in the light of the dawn of a new day, as the New Earth is birthed.

This can feel like a whirlwind that literally whips its way out of what feels like nowhere, and in its wake, your precious, sweet, stable world gets swirled and tossed, while some parts crumble. It is deconstruct to reconstruct time. Remember, everything that was created in the 3D will have to come under review to rise or release, and even if the decision is to rise, the core foundation of it must deconstruct to become new in the higher frequency.

The story of transformation from the caterpillar to the butterfly has been used so often because it truly depicts the process of rebirth, death, new life, and transformation. It is resurrection at its finest. No doubt you know the story well. The caterpillar first winds itself into its cocoon and then secretes fluid that begins to deconstruct its physical form. To do this, it must become present and listen to its natural calling and instinctual response. It trusts its own inner knowing to such a degree that it goes about creating a cocoon and surrendering over to its innate nature. Then it begins to deconstruct itself.

They say that when the caterpillar is in the deconstruction phase, its entire physical being turns to an unrecognizable liquid, and it is an incredibly painful process. When probes have been placed upon the chrysalis, the sounds of moaning and shrieks of pain can be heard with the right equipment. In the middle of the journey, the space in between, the creature that once was and has yet to become is unrecognizable, formless, yet its essence is there awaiting its next expression. There is no doubt that there are moments when the caterpillar believes it is dying or perhaps that it has died. In truth, death and birth are opposite ends of the same experience.

The caterpillar has no choice but to go through the entire process. In time, the cells organize into a new form, yet the DNA stays the same. Cells split and divide, and a new body is created. In time, the chrysalis begins to split, and the butterfly emerges to greet the new world in its unique way. It must pause and dry its wings in the light of the sun. In the perfect time, it takes flight to soar to new heights and explore from an entirely new perspective.

For most, the awakening journey is similar. You know something is happening even if you don't know what it is yet. You find yourself spiraling inward, seeking for clarity. You then begin to deconstruct your internal programmings, such as old limitations, beliefs, and illusions. You start to strip away the external things that no longer match your inner landscape. It is confusing and often painful. It may last for a minute and move through quickly or last for days, weeks, months, and maybe even years. The deconstruction phase is absolutely a necessary phase in this great shift. The more willing you are to surrender, to let go, and to trust, the easier the journey often is. In time, you shall also crack open the chrysalis, emerge new, pause, allow the light to permeate you in your new form, and take flight.

Attach to nothing, allow for everything.

To receive the downloadable BEAUTIFUL SOVEREIGN YOU MEDITATION, please scan this QR code.

Oak Leaf Falling

It is one of those days. The old world is feeling far too dense, and the new is being illusive in its expression through me. This day, like many others during the culmination of ascension, is having its intense way with me. I feel like I am going to explode. I fumble around feeling distorted, off, frustrated, and even angry with all of the 3D density that is seemingly especially loud. I am feeling confused as to what I am supposed to do next, and it seems like every corner I am putting effort in is simply not working.

I know that I need to get away from the computer and into the fresh air, the blazing sun, and the magic of nature. I leave my home and walk to my nearby sacred space, a beautiful meadow with old, winding oak trees offering their arms as a safe haven for me to lie within. They connect me to the earth and give me space and pause to remember.

I decide that before I nestle myself within the trees, I first need to burn off some of the angst energy. I begin by wandering through the meadow and finding feathers, my favorite gifts from the winged animal spirits. I ask to be shown.

The Universe is so generous in her deep well of wisdom given through her offerings. She is always communicating with us through signs, symbols, animals, colors, numbers, songs, and so on. First, though, we must find presence. We must look. We must listen. It is also incredibly potent to ask. As I am walking and beginning to feel the shift in my own consciousness, initiated by that free feeling only nature seems to satisfy, I ask, "What do you most want me to know?"

In a few moments, I find myself coming to a dead stop. I stand still and am summoned to look up. Above me is a beautiful oak tree, not necessarily striking in the sea of oaks around me, but it is summoning my attention all the same. It feels as if all the world is silencing its chatter. My entire focus falls upon one leaf high above. In that still moment, in my full presence and wonder, a gentle wind begins to blow. It brushes across my face and sends my hair dancing about. My gaze is still locked on the upper tree branch, and as I am looking up, one single leaf releases from the tree.

Upon its release, it takes the most beautiful spiraling, sauntering dance upon the gentle breeze. It performs a mesmerizing ballet as it rides on gusts of microcurrents. It takes its time, appearing to be in a splendid journey of joy and absolute freedom. In its own time, it lands a few inches from my feet upon the earth just in front of me.

At that moment, Spirit asks, "Do you see it?" "Yes," I reply. Spirit then asks, "Do you feel it?" "Yes," I say.

Spirit explains, "The leaf is not concerned with what its next step is. It is not in worry or woe. It was sitting there attached to the only expression it had ever known, enjoying the sun and your presence. The leaf felt the summoning of the breeze beneath it and let go without question. It trusted the wind to carry it. It trusted the tree to release it. It did not know where it would go, how it would get there, how it would feel throughout the journey, or even where it would eventually land. It simply let go. It trusted. The leaf landed in the perfect place, in the perfect way, in the perfect moment, as they all do. The leaf knows it shall be carried to where it is to be. It knows that its expression will shift, just as it always has, to how it is meant to express and how it is meant to be. In time, it will churn back into the roots from which it once had been born and will support the journey of creation for eternity. The leaf trusted." Spirit then asks, "Can you?"

In that moment, I am reminded of the perfect cycle of all that has ever been and all that will ever be. Letting go in absolute trust is always perfect and can be a beautiful dance that leads one to the next experience. I know I am the leaf and that all is just as it is meant to be, unfolding in its perfect way, in perfect time. I understand that freedom is always with me, available to be chosen at any moment. I am to be the leaf. I must let go and trust.

Chapter Eight

Breakdown to Breakthrough

"You have to grow from the inside out. None can teach you, none can make you spiritual. There is no other teacher but your own soul."

~ Swami Vivekananda

One of my clients once said, "All of this being present has brought up all of the shit in my life that I needed to see and didn't want to look at. Now I have to deal with it all! This is really not easy. Stop the ride. I want off!" An important part of the awakening process is the breakdown to breakthrough. I have witnessed this happen so many times in myself and in others that I have come to see it as a natural, necessary, and oh-so-uncomfortable part of the transformation to awaken journey.

Once you are in your full presence, you are supersonically aware of what is and what is not working. Then in comes the bittersweet surrender, the letting go alongside the trusting that there is a greater plan moving through you. Through all of this often comes the breakdown.

The breakdown looks different each time it comes, but one thing hums throughout it at every turn. You usually go unconscious and slip temporarily back into the old pain-body and 3D mind-generated way of being. Each time you slip back in, it actually feels worse. You will know you are there because you will conjure up stories and fears of the old to match a current situation. You will likely find yourself spewing negative comments such as: *This always happens. He or she always does this. They are taking everything from me. Etc.* You know you're in a breakdown because it seems catastrophic at the time.

You know from a higher state of consciousness that not one thing is everything, but everything is in each thing. When you are feeling like everything is wrong, you are often in a full-blown pain-body breakdown. The egoic self is also finding its breakdown or deconstruction just in time for its integration at a higher level. This is the pivot point where all ways of being are beginning to change. It is not a straight line to get there. You will rise up and fall down. The swings seem to match in proportion. The higher you rise, the deeper the perceived collapse is experienced. The good news is that it is all temporary. In time, you will rise up and stay right there. The breakdown is for growth. It is essential that you trust the process and do not attach so deeply to it.

My aforementioned client followed her original comment up by asking, "How do I find steady ground?" The answer is that you must first pause. Immense patience is necessary on this ride of becoming new. It is not for the faint of heart.

The key is to identify that you are in a breakdown and become the observer. This is really quite a huge opportunity when you are in a full pain-body breakdown. It can be a challenge or rather an opportunity to see the magic of your life when pushed nose to nose to your pain-body. The pause and the pivot to the observer enables you to Google Earth out, see the bigger picture, and look for all the ways that magic is still very much alive and flowing through you and your life.

During the breakdown, it often feels as if you are going to die in the yuck of the current experience and as if all hope has been lost. It feels so very big because the pain-body and the old way of being are simultaneously screaming to hold their familiar place within you, just as your higher self is reconstructing through you for your next-level healing and frequency rise.

The journey through this massive shift in consciousness is truly like a rollercoaster going up and down, up and down. It is exhausting, even soul-tiring. It is also a very important part of the journey. The opportunity is for you to move into becoming the observer, to find your inner adult, and to also hold your inner child's hand. Yes, this can feel hard, and it is just a moment in time, a snapshot of a very big picture of an amazing and abundant life. Attach to nothing, allow for everything. Becoming the observer gives you the opportunity to experience without drowning in the massive swell of "this is forever-ing."

We are also, on occasion, given the opportunity to walk through our beloveds' breakdowns. My dear friend Natalie had been sharing with me for the past twenty-four hours about how one great plan and deep desire after another had felt as if it was collapsing right in front of her. She was in angst over all the big stuff, such as home, husband, relationships, and purpose. I've witnessed her catastrophizing when she slips into her old pain-body before, as she has witnessed me.

She said, "I feel like a huge steel grate has just scraped through my life." I witnessed her, listened, asked if she could hear a reflection, and gently reminded her that perhaps her pain-body is attaching to old beliefs. Next, I questioned if she had asked her higher self what it would be like if it was all reorganizing for her highest good? She paused, caught her breath, and I could feel her heart calming and mind relaxing into her remembrance. A few hours later, she sent me a few heart emojis with a ton of love and gratitude.

The key in witnessing is to not feed the pain-body but to listen with love because the breakthrough is, no doubt, around the corner. The breakthrough is the rise back up the consciousness scale. It may take a minute, an hour, or even a day, but it always comes. Always! The breakthrough is usually so euphoric that one forgets just how deep in the old pain-body shitstorm they actually were. The one witnessing, however, usually remembers.

The breakthrough brings clarity, the remembrance of power, and connection. You are a sovereign being. The Universe is kind and wants the best for you. Always! If the breakdown is going unconscious in the 3D, then the breakthrough is your rise up to the super-soul-powered 5D, to you as Source-consciousness remembrance. The interesting thing about the breakthrough is that it does not always require resolve from the thing or things that led you to the breakdown. It isn't situational. It is vibrational. The same scenarios may be at play, but you are no longer playing with them in the same way. You remembered who you are, raised your frequency back up, are now looking for solutions and possibilities, and you feel magnificent. The breakthrough can be such a massive rise up in frequency that it leaves you feeling incredible, often better than before you took the unconscious dive into breakdown land.

During the process of awakening, this swing seems to happen every few days, but not alway as the big shock of catastrophe, thank all that is holy. It is more of an up and down, mini breakdown-to-breakthrough frequency, woven with the massive kabooms that feel like they take you out momentarily, but then voilà you rise up again shiny, polished, and new, feeling whole, sourced, and unstoppable.

Chapter Nine
Rise or Release

"Some of us think holding on makes us strong,
but sometimes it is letting go."

~ Herman Hesse

This journey is not for the faint of heart, and you have all of the tools alive within you to move through this awakening process. There is, however, a moment along the journey where you have reached a point of your own ascension where everything, and I mean everything, must come up for review. You are rising up in frequency, and most of what you have created in the past was created from an old lens, from desires that matched the growth cycle you were in at that time. Most of what you have created was created through 3D density, playing through the pain-body's desire to heal or even to spiral in the pain to feel connected. Remember, you entered this earth plane to ride through the old ride of karma, your soul's lessons and agreements, to heal through contrast, and to rise up and remember. It is now time to rise up in remembrance.

Everything is taken into account and into a state of analysis or inventory. This includes your thoughts, words, feelings, home, job, habits, beliefs, relationships, state or even country, possibly even how you present yourself through your voice and appearance. Seriously, everything must come under the microscope for review. You cannot pull any one edge of this matrix without pulling it all. You do not change one expression of yourself without a ripple of change moving through each of your expressions.

You would never polish one facet of a diamond without polishing the entire gem to greater brilliance, never ever. You are awakening to your pure crystalline lightbody. You are becoming the multifaceted, perfectly cut, insanely valuable, pure-light diamond, and everything else must rise in your light or be released in time.

This indeed can be one of the most difficult and perhaps painful parts of this entire journey to awakening. Not everyone or everything rises together at the same time or in the same way. Some will rise up in a different timeline sequence, while others simply may not rise at all. You get to review it all, not from the mind of what you "should" do, not from the fear positioning of scarcity or lack, but rather from your cellular truth of higher consciousness and soul's guidance as to what is and what is no longer for you. No, this is not easy. Yes, it can and must all be done with truth, grace, and love.

Your own internal review of who you are being begins in your inner plane. Do your words match your desires? Are you speaking positively of and to yourself? And of and to others? Are you holding your highest frequency no matter what is bumping or crashing into you? Oh yes, it will all come crashing up against you at some point. Are you operating from your truest knowing? Are you speaking your truth and encouraging others to do the same?

Let's look at relationships. The parental agreement was one of soul-contract fulfillment. We have already discussed the karma play. Intimate relationships, especially long-term ones, were also often created from an old expression of need and desire that may now be complete within you as you rise up in your remembrance. Relationships are reviewed by what frequency they hold and how they leave you feeling.

Questions regarding relationships must be asked of your higher self. How do your energy bodies meet? How do you feed each other emotionally, spiritually? Are you growing together or apart? Are you stuck in old, familiar patterns? Do you both have a desire to rise up together? Are you even speaking the same language? Do you leave feeling better for having been engaged with one another?

The old frequency of relationship agreements from the 3D lens was to fulfill soul contracts, give the greatest opportunity for growth, and to mirror the wounds and pain points of the other to inspire healing and remembrance of soul truth. It has been very common to find connection through pain or loss. Of course, no one sees this in the beginning. Your love-drunk souls dance in delight as intoxicating frequencies pour over you. You see the other's light and feel his or her resonances. You are both overjoyed to have found the "perfect match."

In time, you begin to realize that there are some shadowy things to look at, and next comes the "Oh wait, this may be a bit more than I had realized." From the 3D lens, people are usually attracted through pain points that are eventually revealed to ultimately be healed. The frequency of the 5D, on the other hand, shifts the entire matrix of relationships. In this higher frequency, you will meet and join from your light-bodies, no longer from your pain-bodies.

In the higher frequency, you are whole, sovereign, healed, full, connected to everything and everyone. Relationships from this place become a mirror of wholeness, as a complete expression of I AM

Whole! You are whole, and together you stand in each of your unique and fully recognized sovereignty. No one completes another in 5D relating. You are complete, and the soul standing in front of you is complete. Together you stand as two in unity. Can you see from this perspective how everything also needs to change? In the 5D, there is no longing, there is no pain, there is only love, allowance, presence, grace, and God. That is where you are rapidly heading. It is time to lay down the sword of suffering and rise up in the power of truest soul expression to create this new reality.

Important to note is that when one soul remembers sooner than the other, the dynamics of the relationship will shift. When one is still playing, vibrating, and expressing the 3D pain-body of fear and lack, it can feel heavy and dense, and this often translates into control issues. When the other has risen in his or her truest birthright of sovereignty, there is a gap in the frequency between the two. A bridge can absolutely be built, and eventually most, if not all, will rise. However, for some the preferred choice is to release the relationship if the frequency is weighing down the expansion to new heights.

Many intimate friend relationships, especially for women, were created in the old density based on commiseration of the pain-body. The program of the old is to feed the pain and connect through alikeness. One woman listens to the other's pain, then identifies her own pain, then shares that back so the sister doesn't feel so alone. This old program, for what seems like an eternity, was considered to be bonding and called friendship.

"You think that's bad? Listen to this!" I can feel those words in my throat, as I had said them so often in connection with friends in the old density. As you rise up, your friend bonds must rise up, too. Can you witness a friend in pain and create space to listen without needing to identify with or bring it back to your own mirror of pain?

To sit with another, to listen, and to witness is a potent practice and a higher-dimensional way of connecting and communicating.

When the pain-body is rearing its head, it heals by being witnessed, not matched. It is important to set parameters for this. A conscious friend will appreciate the parameters. Perhaps you offer a time for her pain-body to dump. I am a huge fan of the number eleven, so eleven minutes. Ready? Set? Go! Look deeply into her eyes and allow her to purge her pain-body through words, gestures, screams, tears, or movement. At the end of the eleven minutes, everyone takes a breath, shakes it off, grounds, and realigns. You can then offer a reflection such as, "I witness how hard, scary, painful, (etc.) this is for you."

Next, there is an opportunity to transmute the energy and move it up the emotion scale. You could tell her that you know how powerful she is, that you've watched her create miracles over and over again, and that one is, no doubt, coming now too. You can keep bringing the light of her soul's truth back in front of her so that she can also remember. This is not to deny or dismiss her pain but to let it find its release without attachment through the power of remembrance of just exactly who she is at soul level. This is the consciousness shift.

Not all relationships will rise with you. Let us remember the programming of the 3D mind and its attachment to pain. If your beloved friend of twenty years isn't yet ready to "Rise Sister Rise!" with you, then maybe she is not be able to join you on the ladder of ascension at this time. It is not for you to convince her but for you to lead by presence and example. If she is on the cusp of her own awakening, she will see you, actually she will feel your transformation, and the light of her own being will have her lean more deeply into the light, like a moth to the flame.

When you are ready to rise and awaken, it often only takes a few opportunities of sensing the new energy for others to stop and say, "I'll have what she's having!" A significant level of patience is required in this process, however. There is also, at times, a tipping point where the gap between where you were and where you are going simply becomes so significant that maybe the expanse is just too wide to traverse. This is where the release occurs.

Release is different for everyone. I recently had a friend of twenty-seven years release our relationship without even a conversation. Her pain-body was feeling unsupported, and yet I was unaware, as it had not been communicated with me. It was shocking initially, painful in many ways, and then there was a beautiful surrender into the allowance and understanding from a dimensional-shift perspective. I released her with love. In time we found our way back to each other. We walked through a very powerful expansion together as we both were initiated by the power of death in a short period of time.

If your friend is used to meeting in the commiseration-station frequency, and you stop playing the game, her pain-body will get loud, it will scream, beg, and stir up even more pain. It is essential to walk people forward, lead by example, and steer the conversation in a direction that does feel good to you. Often they will pick up the frequency and walk with you. If not, you may find yourself slowly backing away, becoming less and less available. Boundaries, the big, beautiful, next-level players, can then be set.

Ah yes, boundaries! Boundaries are used not to push relationships away but to give clear indicators as to how to be in a good standing relationship and bring people closer. At some point, if the walk into higher communion isn't working, then you will have an amazing opportunity to speak your truth. You could explain that you've been going through a ton of changes, and share that you are making choices in every expression of your life to rise up to a new light, or even simply express that you are committed to focusing on the positive and creating more of that.

You could even invite your friend to join you and play a new game as an experiment. You could begin with suggesting, "Let's choose to only share what's working well for the next twenty minutes and then expand upon that." If this experiment does not work, you may need to set firmer boundaries and express clearly that you are looking to support a rise up in power instead of sitting in the woe and pain of the old discomforts. If this is not met in a way that feels good for you, the next step is to shift how much time you are spending together. This is the Rise or Release.

In the new, you are new. Everything that is a part of you is being asked to become new right alongside you. As I was writing this, I was also living this. My friend stepped back from our friendship, at the same time I was also looking at our home going up for sale and questioning my own long-term relationships.

What I experienced within myself was a collapse into the old 3D way of being. I must say it was perhaps the most uncomfortable period of time I had walked through in at least a decade. Every edge was being pulled, and I fell into my old programming! I had forgotten who I was and all that I had learned as an "awakening-in-consciousness" human who had been teaching hundreds. I had forgotten my own truth.

I went completely unconscious and fell face-first into the 3D matrix of fear, lack, and pain, and I so badly wanted others to commiserate with me on the "oh-ain't-it-awful" playground. I was even mad that one friend had danced over my pain share and went straight to her own winning truth. Not one of my friends would commiserate with me, not one! They all listened and said, "I know it is all going to work out perfectly. It always does."

My friends would not match me where I was, and I was pissed. So, I moved deeper into my own well and started scurrying about trying to make something happen, to hurry up and find another place to live, even if it was temporary. I scurried in fear, feeling more and more awful! Instead of presence, pause, faith, and trust, I was reactive, angry, crying uncontrollably. I was in my own created hell.

Then one day, about a few weeks in, I woke back up and remembered who I was, who I had moved heaven to earth in my own remembrance to become. I stopped! I paused and lifted my head up and literally said out loud to myself, "I Am a Fucking Creator! What Do I Want?" And yes, it was one of those moments where the clouds parted as the light streamed through. I have no doubt that the angels and The Light Council were singing on high. In that moment, I remembered, and everything became crystal clear.

I said no to three different things I was juggling to try to appease my fear, to two possible houses that I knew were not for me, and to a business opportunity that I had no bandwidth for at that moment. I picked up my phone and said, "No. No. No, Thank You." Boom. The next few moments were an absolute rush. I felt my power come back, my frequency rise, and in less than a minute, I was remembered.

I could see clearly that I was to ask for what I wanted, trust in the unknown, take pause and await the next steps to be clearly shown to me, and to see what magic was unfolding.

You choose each moment, first for yourself. Will you rise up to the remembrance of you as a conscious creator whom your soul has always known? Will you release the old and be one in co-creation with Source? Or, will you attach to the old familiar distorted lens of suffering and fear-based reaction? You choose over and over again until the choice becomes so natural that the old programs are forever released with absolutely no access to going back.

It is all here for you, as it always has been. The curtains are parting so you can see the truth. You are the creator of it all, and it is always working out for your greatest joy and highest good.

Chapter Ten
The Pain-Body Meets the Higher Self

"For love to flourish, the light of your presence needs to be strong enough so that you no longer get taken over by the thinker or the pain-body and mistake them for who you are. To know yourself as the Being underneath the thinker, the stillness underneath the mental noise, the love and joy underneath the pain, is freedom, salvation, enlightenment."

~ Eckhart Tolle

According to spiritual author Eckhart Tolle, the old emotional pain that is carried around with a person is called the "pain-body." You know the pain-body well, although you may not yet identify it as such. The pain-body aligns and often expresses through the egoic self, as it anchors itself fully within the emotional body and expresses itself through the mind as thoughts that trigger or enhance an emotional response and reaction.

Let us remember that 3D is the expression of the mind, the place where the pain-body has created its home. As one awakens, a shift must occur within the pain-body and the egoic self. The pain-body deeply fears your higher consciousness activation because it believes that it will die if or rather when you rise in frequency and ascend into 5D awareness.

In some ways this is true. There is often an experience of death of parts of yourself as you are becoming new. I like to assure the pain-body that it is less about dying and more about integrating into a new expression. This supports the process at a much higher level and gives all of the expressions of you a smoother journey forward.

I also believe that entities of lower frequency attach themselves through the pain-body and feed upon the lower frequency that one omits when in fear, despair, and even anger. This makes it an extra fun journey of elevation. Not only are you navigating programs of the mind, ancestral pain-body remembrance held in your DNA, as well as the imprints of the world around you, but you must also now deal with entities that attach like parasites.

I was shown in meditation that attaching entities are similar in many ways to the bacteria living in your gut, commonly known as candida. If you have ever had an overgrowth of this bacteria, then you know just how much havoc it can wreak over your entire body and well-being. Candida lives within the gut. We need a little bit of it to create balance in the flora, to assist in the breaking down and assimilation of foods, and to aid in the absorption of nutrients.

When candida gets overgrown due to stress, antibiotics, poor diet, etc., a multitude of problems in your physical body appear. Candida lives on sugar. The remedy is to starve it and your body of sugar and to bring in more of the good bacteria to override the bad. After a few days of this, it will begin to die. Here is the thing, candida does not want to die, just as the pain-body and the entities attached to it do not want to die.

Candida will emit a chemical from itself that travels to your brain and says, "Eat Sugar!" It wants to ensure its survival. Similarly, entities and the pain-body itself emits a frequency and conjures up memories and scenarios that have your head spinning into the lower "oh-ain't-it-awful" density. You find yourself future projecting over how it's all going to go, and it's usually going to hell in a perfectly woven handbasket of familiarity when the pain-body is activated and fighting for its very alive place within you.

The more people heal and expand, the louder the old programs and the pain-body gets, it seems. Here is why. Just like candida, if you can set your intention and commitment to being well and not giving into the old way of being, if you choose to not eat the sugar, in a very short time the overgrowth will die away, the rest will integrate into balance, and voilà you are back in homeostasis and well-being.

How you "starve" the pain-body is by finding neutral. In any moment, with any situation, can you find the grace of neutrality? The situation at hand may be the same, but you can choose to be neutral in the face of it. It is often way too hard to go from fear straight to trust or love, to move from anger straight to forgiveness, shame straight to ease. You can, however, stair step your way there, and you will eventually become so familiar with being neutral that it will feel like a breath, a pause point. You then, over time, move from neutral to light, ease, trust, joy, balance, love, and ultimately to peace.

You must first become fiercely present and catch every single thought. You can then begin to guide your thoughts back to presence and to what you ARE willing to experience. You have to reprogram your thoughts, choose only well-being, and deny and dismiss the destructive desire of fear and pain. As you raise your vibration up to love, the pain-body, in time, relaxes and begins to rise up in frequency, and the entities fall away.

The pain-body is loud, so very loud. It is no doubt the loudest voice in your room. It loves to fight for its right to suffer. It fights for the deeply embedded, well-formed limitations. It does this by seeking proof of just how awful it all is and just how much worse it will, no doubt, become. When we are inspired to move up the vibrational scale, the pain-body says, "Yes, but...." "Yes, but Lisa, you don't understand how awful he is, it is, you are ... how in the red your bank account is ... how hard it is!" If I only had a dollar for each time I was sitting with a master being who suggested the possibilities beyond lack and limitation and for how many "Yes, buts" I have heard in response, even said by myself.

It is a program of lack, limitation, pain, and suffering. No, it is not your fault, nor is it your natural state. Your soul knows you are not, nor have ever been, here to suffer. It has all been learned, programmed, and imprinted. The program is then protected, encouraged, and fought for so it has the right to be and stay the loudest voice in the room. Are you tired yet? Exhausted even?

The pivot comes when you are no longer willing to suffer at your own hand or rather mind. It arrives when you hit the bottom, exhausted, bloodied, and bruised to then one day wake up to realize it has been you the entire time. You come to know that nothing is ever happening to you but rather through you. In that moment of realization, you get to choose to Rise and Shine or sit in the pain-body and suffer some more.

When a crow is being aggressive with a bald eagle to protect its nest or steal the eagle's food, the crow will often jump on the eagle's back and fly along with the magnificent beast. The eagle will do its best to dismantle the tag-along bird by making rapid turns mid-flight, often to no avail. The eagle then begins to ascend to new heights, higher and higher it flies. In time, the eagle will soar to such an altitude that the crow can no longer breathe in oxygen and will fall off of the eagle's back. The higher you soar into light, the harder it will be for the old programs, pain-body responses, and entities that feed upon them to hold on.

As you awaken in remembrance, the old becomes less and less comfortable, and you will choose, in time, to stay in your light and your higher frequency of love. When the pain-body is loud, talk to it like a child in pain. When children fall down on the playground, the first thing they do is look around for those who witnessed their tumble in an attempt to garner sympathy for their pain. When mothers or care providers are found, tears begin to fall, and children are usually picked up and soothed with kind words such as, "Oh honey, I am sorry that you're hurt," and actions such as knees being brushed off and then kissed. With such attention and comfort, children are up and running in no time. All pain, especially the pain that was experienced or imprinted in your youth, responds and often heals from simply being acknowledged, soothed over with love, and set free for the next higher expression.

When your pain-body is loud, catch it before it overtakes you. Acknowledge the pain: *Wow, that is scary. That was hard. This is familiar, like when A, B, or C happened.* Your being would not respond with fear or angst if there wasn't the first and original wound, held in a program or memory, that is being triggered. Find the original wound and offer acknowledgement to that part of you still holding on to the memory as if it was yesterday: *I am so sorry that (insert memory) happened. Pain-body, I acknowledge that you are scared, hurting, feeling abandoned, (whatever is true).* Take a deep breath and choose another expression: *Even though this is hard, I know I am powerful and that everything is always working out for my greatest good and highest joy.* Then sit in that truth until you reach a new height, until the old falls away.

This is a process, as is everything. It can shift as soon as you decide you have suffered enough and are absolute in your willingness to awaken to remember that you are a master creator living an earth-plane experience. Nothing ever happens to you but is created through you. At any moment it is for your choosing to rise up, change your mind, shift to a higher frequency, and expect the miracles that are here humming along on a parallel track of the pain.

It is all here for you. You are the creator of every experience you have ever lived through. Your freedom is alive within you, and your soul wants nothing more than for you to shine in your greatest light, while allowing love and service to this earth and humanity to fill your every breath. You are here to awaken the consciousness of humanity, and it begins here and now. With this breath, this blink of your eye, you choose.

LIGHT COUNCIL CHANNEL

"As the journey of dimension shifting and becoming new is massively upon you, there is undoubtedly a significant amount of pressure being placed upon you, the likes of which you have never experienced before in such volume or consistency. You feel the effects of this in every expression of your living. As was said earlier, everything is up for review. Everything created in the 3D lens must rise up or release. This includes the very structure of your being.

This is a time like no other. We commend you for your willingness, your conviction, and your commitment to this journey. Your soul has chosen well, and this will, no doubt, go down in earth's history as being one of the most significant transformational times that has ever been experienced on the earth plane.

We want to bring a greater awareness to you as to what is happening within the cells of your bodies. You have been operating in flesh form as a carbon expression. Your cells and atoms are made up of carbon, as is much of what you experience in your earth-plane reality. Part of the journey that you are currently undergoing is a massive transformation of the very core of your construction. You are becoming light!

Think of the diamond and how it is created. Carbon is held through force for a significant amount of time until there is a shift in its molecular structure. An alchemy occurs, transforming that carbon block into a crystalline expression. In time, this alchemy creates a new form, and although the diamond in its rawest form may not bring you joy immediately as you gaze upon it, with some finessing and polishing, you are shown a spectacular spectrum of pure crystalline light. This diamond is known as one of the strongest compounds on earth. The pressure which you are experiencing is actually having a similar effect upon your cellular structures. You are being compressed to transform.

Your carbon form is turning to crystalline light. And in time, with some polishing and finessing, you will also awaken to the phenomenal display of you as the diamond, multifaceted, sustainable, strong and vital, reflective of all light prisms, and shining an infinite light.

There is so much happening within and around you, dearest one, so much so that your mind cannot begin to understand. We urge you to release the limitations of your mind, allow the alchemy to fully occur, and celebrate your diamond self. You are the light of a thousand stars compressed into a living, breathing expression. You are extraordinary beyond measure, and now is your time."

- The Light Council

Pillar Four
ASCENSION

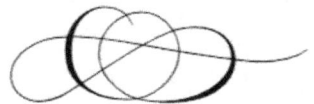

The Morning

I finally arrived "home" just a few hours after the sun rose. I am deeply in shock, delirious, exhausted, confused, and numb, yet somehow not. It will be an hour or so before my team of "handlers" arrives, my sacred soul sisters who hold me in all of the ways and do not leave my side for several days. I sit up tall even though the deepness of my down couch wants to pull me in. I feel him calling me again. "It's going to be alright," I tell him, "you're dead." I pause, hearing my voice attempting to take the truth of this in myself while simultaneously innocently trying to convince him of the same truth. "Just like I told you in the hospital," I continue, "Tim, you are dead!" "You can hear me?" he whispers through the veils. "LISA YOU CAN HEAR ME?" he then screams through the ethers. "I can hear you," I say. "That's fucking amazing," he replies.

In the decade and a half we had been together, Tim knew, but he never really knew how deeply the connection between myself and the spirit world I played in went. I never imagined that these gifts that had come in with my birth were going to play out as they were in this moment. "You are going to be okay," I say, "I now need you to let me know that our son and I will also be okay." "I am sorry," he responds. Then silence. Then "I love you." This rings through my head, my heart, and my soul. This "I love you" rings deeper than any other "I love you" has before. It is like the bell of truth that rang in heaven on the day he left his body behind, and it will never stop ringing through my being as the truth. "I Love You!"

Chapter Eleven
Remembrance

"And above all, watch with glittering eyes the whole world around you because the greatest secrets are always hidden in the most unlikely places. Those who don't believe in magic will never find it."

~ Roald Dahl

You have no doubt heard someone say, "My awakening happened four years ago," or ten, twenty, or whenever might be true for that certain person. It is not uncommon for people to point to a particular experience or event that began to turn their consciousness to a higher level. It absolutely can occur like that, and for others, it is a series of events or experiences over time that supports their consciousness to turn a corner and rise up to the next level. There is no "right" way to do this awakening journey. Your soul knows. Your soul always knows.

For many, the pandemic, which unfolded as this book was being written, was a massive turning point to a next level of awakening. It is important to understand that awakening takes on many expressions. There are many levels of awakening that play out in both the inner and the outer planes, in both your personal world and the global world at large. You cannot pull one edge of this spider's web we call consciousness without pulling the entire matrix along with it.

I have naively spent most of my life focused entirely on the inner awakening of consciousness. Now I see so clearly how this must also play out on the global stage. I, as well as many, have awakened to the next level of understanding regarding the truth of what has been at the core of the operating systems on planet earth for far too long. The awakening is pouring through each human being in a very personal and unique way. It must also play through all of the current systems for humanity to truly rise up to the light of the 5D heaven-on-earth expression, the expression that your soul said "Yes!" to before coming here in physical form.

I have experienced several fundamental leaps, or awakenings, along the ascension scale or spiritual ladder over this lifetime, as I know you have as well. In my earlier years, they would terrify me. Fortunately, now when they come, although they still hold a significant kabam, there is much less fear attached to them. With the rapid fire of ascension that is upon us, you can expect to experience a leap or two yourself probably within the time it has taken you to read these words.

Leaps up the spiritual ladder of ascension always look different but hold a similar imprint. You will know something otherworldly has just occurred and that everything has somehow shifted in response. It is not always easy to put words to the experience, as this is an inside journey of consciousness that leaves a lasting impression of transformation alive within you.

One of my leaps happened on the day after Easter of 2021. I was making the bed, a very "normal" daily routine. There's nothing so magical about making a bed, or so I thought. As it first began, I experienced what felt like remembering pieces of a dream. It was like when little snippets of memory come back to you, and as you follow the memories, you begin to remember bits and pieces, not always in any sort of logical order, but it starts coming back to you. This is how it began, like remembering a dream. The distorting part was that I knew it wasn't a dream I had just dreamt. It was like memories of a hundred dreams that came flooding through in high-speed succession. I couldn't really hold on to or even make sense of much of what I was "remembering." It was like a rapid-fire sequence of many pieces of a dream. It was very surreal. I started to feel as if I was in an awake dream myself, still making the bed, but absolutely not feeling connected to earth-plane reality.

I was guided to sit in the comfy chair in my bedroom, you know the chair that no one ever really sits in, the one that holds clothes more often than bodies. I cleared the chair of its contents, and as I sat, I felt myself being whisked up, and up, and then up some more. The Light Council had come forth and was telling me that they were bringing back my soul memory banks, flecks of myself and memories from thousands of years ago. It was not for my mind to make sense of, which did not even seem possible, but rather for soul integration, the holding of memories of many other places, dimensions, and experiences. (Such soul remembrance is what is available to us as the old 3D is collapsing.)

I found myself there for possibly one or maybe two hours. Actually, I honestly have no idea how long I was there, as it was such an other-worldly, out-of-body experience. They showed me a timeline that spanned an eighty-day period. They assured me that the journey over the next eighty days would be significant, that all of my soul parts needed to come back online in actualized time in order to integrate the higher expressions and dimensions of self, and that all I was experiencing was preparation for what was to come. They were not kidding!

I listened, I cried, I flowed with the frequency, and eventually I "came to." I was happy to have had the time to be there, which was also divine, as my schedule had completely changed earlier in the day. Everything is always perfectly imperfect, is it not? Afterward, there was a fundamental shift in all of my reality. I have no clear exact memories of it all but rather a sense of greater wholeness and a next level of "knowing."

Since that experience, I have become increasingly aware that, as we are expanding so rapidly to the next level of expression, we will eventually be spending most of our time in this fully expanded state. We will be living the dream while in the dream at the same time, the dream of our souls' remembrance and greatest dance, rising somehow just above our old expressions, just a little higher up, like the ethers of heaven dancing through in an increasingly consistent manner, remembering us as a heavenly beings of light to bring this remembrance to our earth-plane reality. This gives us an uncanny opportunity to be somewhat detached yet oddly present in the same moment.

This is the movement beyond the mind and into greater soul expression. It is dreamy and offers an oddly untethered attachment to who, what, where, when, and even how any of this earth-plane reality plays out. You are walking up a ladder of ascension. You must know this no matter what you are experiencing. You are a human on planet earth and are the most revered of all of the soul expressions in all of the galaxies. Souls are standing in line to be here for the greatest show the earth has ever seen, and you are here in soul consciousness expressing as flesh, blood, and bone, feeling it all, being both the observer and the creator.

You are ascending so rapidly, and it is important to understand that the leaps are often experienced as if you are skipping a few rungs of the spiritual ladder. Yes, there are moments when you will step back down a rung or two while you are finding your steady footing, just as there are also the precious moments in time when you will experience a massive ascension. The key, when these leaps arrive, is to make a conscious decision to trade any fear you may have for curiosity, anticipation, and an open heart so that you may fully enjoy the journey.

After each step, and absolutely after each leap, it is essential that you find your new normal and some steady ground while everything in, of, and around you begins to find a new normal as well. These high flying experiences will integrate and normalize within you, as your job is to bring heaven to earth, and each step brings you to the next height, a greater connection, and the next level of soul remembrance.

These leaps up the ladder happen to everyone. They are experienced in whatever way is best for you, given where you are and what your soul agreements are. There is no wrong or right way to do any of this, just as there is no avoiding the ascension experience. This is what you agreed to, it is what you were made for, and each step up the ladder is bringing you home to your greatest self.

The Bench

It is a day like many during this massive shift of awakening. I am feeling incredibly uncomfortable and know that the fresh air, sun, and my favorite trees are calling me to them. As I walk around the meadow near my home, I truly allow myself to surrender over to nature, to its magic and messages, in a way I rarely give myself the space to do while indoors. The winter sun is already setting behind the mountain just a bit before four in the afternoon. All that I really want is to find a comfortable place to sit, so the sun can touch my face, while I touch the earth. As I turn the corner, I see a bench positioned so perfectly beneath the wide reaching oak. Weathered yet sturdy, it was there summoning me towards it. I have walked this same loop through the meadow many, many times over the years, even just the week before, and this bench was never there. I feel like I am being given the most beautiful gift. There it is, just for me. I make my way over to it and sit with the last rays of sun on my face. I weep.

The pressure of the discomfort I have been feeling finally pours forth. I say, "Thank you, thank you, thank you for this gift." Spirit replies, "I am always providing for you. All of it is here for you. Just ask." I have remembrance in this moment.

Truly we are one. Everything we want, need, and desire is here for us. I asked and released it over without another thought, and there was magic awaiting me. The feeling of connection in this remembrance was just what I needed to get back to a place that felt good and to a vibration that was more aligned with who I was becoming.

Such a potent reminder is shown to you each and every day if you are truly in presence, surrender, trust, and allowance. It is the magic of divine co-creation with Source.

Everything is here for you. Just ask. There is a universal law that the benevolent forces cannot interfere with your free will. This includes your angels, guides, ascended masters, ancestors, divine beings of light, and the galactic community. Even as they are gathered all around you, they cannot jump in to shift your experience of reality in any way without first being given permission. You give permission by asking "please" and by expressing gratitude with a "thank you." The only time they are able to override your experience is if your life is in danger and it is not your soul's agreed upon time to exit your body. You've heard the stories of the car spinning out of control, about to plummet off the edge, when suddenly a miracle occurs, and the car is stopped by unseen forces.

How you co-create with the Universe is by asking, releasing expectations, staying present, and awaiting your gifts. This is a super power that every human possesses, yet few are utilizing. Play with creation.

Ask for what you want. Act as if a miraculous gift awaits for you just around the next corner, and it will, in fact, show itself to you. The key is non-attachment to form or timing. Simply trust!

Ask for everything, all day long, every day! And offer gratitude for all that has appeared and all that is coming. Be sure to also ask that it all arrives in the best way possible, with ease, and for your greatest joy and highest good. When I first started playing with angels and guides, I wanted proof, so I began this co-creative manifesting journey by asking for feathers and pennies to fall from heaven. I would ask often with a bit of "show me this is real" energy. I also trusted because I so very badly wanted to believe. The miracles that then unfolded were truly stunning. I would find pennies and feathers in the most unique and unimaginable places. I even had a feather appear in my shower one day! What?!?

Each time I received one of these gifts, I would receive it fully, pick it up, and give thanks. In time, I moved on to bigger things like parking spaces. OMG, I have become a quantum parking space creator. One of my favorite creations was when I was attending a workshop in San Francisco. It was the usual busy downtown San Fran at dinner time, and a group of us were headed to a restaurant. We had been driving around for 15 minutes trying to find a parking spot. "Wait!" I exclaimed. "Let's create together. Let's all put our hearts together and ask for a miraculous rock star parking place!" It was literally two minutes later when the perfect parking space opened up right in front of the restaurant, literally at the front door. It was a rock star parking moment, and there have been many more since then.

I figured, if it works for these smaller things, then why not aim a little higher? The journey of creating as if by magic has become a true blessing and miracle in my life, and each time the creation appears, I give thanks. The key when beginning this journey is to start small with the things that seem insignificant, as you are neutral in the asking. It is not as easy to ask for the big, emotionally triggered things right out of the gate because your pain-body is often not yet ready to find the neutral ground or align vibrationally with the thing you desire. If it was, it would already be with you. Start small and expand into bigger things as you are remembered to your power with Source and are truly moving into the embodiment that you are a divine creator.

The Universe is a magnificent playground here to delight you in all the ways. It is you who has forgotten your power. The Universe and all of the beings who are part of the universal playground have been here all along awaiting your awakening to remember.

Enjoy the bounty and give gratitude for all things.

Chapter Twelve
Ascension Symptoms

"Within you lies the opportunity to grow in spirit. Keep your feet on the earth, but lift your face towards the heavens. Surrender to the light with a tranquil mind and a heart full of the love of God."

~ White Eagle

This journey of becoming NEW also has many physical expressions and opportunities for you to move through. You are most likely experiencing or have already experienced many ascension symptoms along your journey of awakening. Some are finding, as they move through the density of the old and align more and more freely to the higher frequency of the new, that these symptoms increase for a period of time, sometimes becoming unbearable.

Many find great relief in trusting that there isn't necessarily something physically wrong with them, but that the symptoms are just part of the journey, as the old, dense carbon matter gives way for the crystalline lightbody to emerge. Many have sought medical support and found nothing medically wrong. It is always advised, however, to seek medical assistance if your symptoms continue to increase or become intolerable.

In the next chapter, there are tools for navigating your energy body which may assist in easing some of these symptoms so that you can find relief as integration occurs. I have observed these symptoms in myself and in countless others. Sometimes they massively increase, then integrate with time, and relief is felt.

Headaches

Tension in the head and neck is a very common ascension symptom. There is a significant amount of pressure building up within the pineal gland as it begins to decalcify. The calcification has occurred over many eons of toxicity building up on the earth. Currently there are chemicals such as fluoride and even bleach being added to the waters, and countless pesticides and other chemicals are contaminating the soils. Processed foods are made predominantly of chemicals and are massively consumed at this time. Even the air you breathe is filled with impurities. All of this leads to calcification of the pineal gland. Some believe this is all intentional and devised by dark forces upon planet earth in order to keep humanity in its slumber, ticking along asleep. It is time to wake up, my friend, and here we are.

The pineal gland is believed to be the chemical expression of your divine connection to Source, as well as the source of your intuitive knowledge. The pressure in this gland can also come from the chakral shifts occurring through your energy body, as the crown and third eye must open for higher alignment and integration. This pressure can be very intense at times.

Body Aches and Pains

The entire structure of your human expression is transforming as you become more of a crystalline lightbody expression. The density of the old must make way for the lightness of the new. This also must play out in your physical body expression. The energy of your body must flow outward to allow for the new energy sequences to emerge. I have found that most ascension pain occurs in the neck, but it is not exclusively held there.

Also, when emotional pain is left unattended over long periods of time, it begins to manifest into physical form, causing pain or eventually disease. All physical ailments can be traced back to an emotional experience.

The body is like an amazing map or a puzzle. When you know the code of what each organ, region, and physical expression aligns to, you can then begin to decipher what emotion or experience is held there. This is a combination of Chinese medicine, intuition, and mapping the body's wisdom I have gathered while working as a healer with thousands of physical bodies over many decades. Louise Hay was one of the early explorers to map the emotional story through the physical body.

You are also processing through your physical body the pain, trauma, and contracts of your ancestors. Have you ever noticed the familial patterns or sequences handed down through family lines? Yes, genetics can play a role, but some things in familial patterns simply cannot be explained away, like when a person marries at the same age as his or her mother or father and then divorces in just as many years later. Look for patterns, as they are completing and moving through your physical form. The resulting aches and pains can be navigated by increasing water intake, taking epsom salt baths, and participating in purification rituals.

The pain in the neck can be a metaphor for all the pressure upon you as you strip away the old 3D density. Are you carrying the world on your shoulders? When I began channeling, the entry point for information was the crown of my head and the base of my skull, the sixth and seventh chakra points. I do believe that these points have to adjust to the massive new frequency of energy that is pouring in. Opening to expand, all of this is playing out through your physical human structure.

Ringing and Popping in the Ears

Along with headaches, ringing and popping in the ears seems to be the most common ascension symptom. The ringing lasts for seconds or even minutes. In my experience, popping is one of the first steps, and it feels like going under water. In time, for me, it became an indicator that a new energy being was present and wanting to make contact.

With ringing in the ears, the pitch often seems to change. The frequency of the ringing seems to match with the Schumann resonance patterns of gamma light band frequency flooding the planet. Ringing in my ears began several years ago and would occur initially as I was doing energy work with clients. It now seems to become more and more consistent as the ascension frequencies increase. There are moments when it becomes so intense that I actually have to stop what I am doing, close my eyes, take a breath, and ride through it.

It has been shown that our ear chakras are being upgraded to a supersonic frequency of hearing. Remember that part of ascension is feeling more. All of your senses have to come online and turn up to the next level in order to elevate you as a sentient being.

Vertigo/Dizziness

The sheer number of people reporting an increase in vertigo has gotten my attention. Vertigo is when the crystals that live within the ear canal dislodge and begin to float through the ocular tunnel. It is an incredibly uncomfortable experience when it occurs, as the room spins uncontrollably for a period of time. In the worst cases, one may even vomit from the experience. There are several exercises that support aligning the crystals back into their proper placement, and a simple Google search will lead you to them.

After experiencing a few particularly unpleasant rounds of vertigo, The Light Council showed me that the inner ear crystals were themselves being upgraded. They need to expand in frequency and size, they said, to support the next level of receptivity of collective vibrational frequency and to increase our ability to "hear" the messages from on high that are communicating and activating greater intuitive knowing.

Sleep

It is very common to have sleep disruptions during massive ascension frequency upgrades. The mind is being reprogrammed or actually deprogrammed at times. It seems that sleeplessness comes in a sequence, usually lasting a few days. If you are experiencing this, please be sure to see what the moon phase is doing. It is more common to experience insomnia during full moon periods.

The Light Council has shared that upgrades must occur as part of the soul agreements at this time. They have said that if they are not given the space needed to upgrade during waking hours, then the upgrades will have to occur at night. To give way during the day, one must move into a meditative state and open both the root and crown chakras, the heaven to earth portal.

Much of this does occur while you are sleeping, but as the new frequencies enter, it can alert the system and cause you to awaken. If you experience sleeplessness, it is in fact a great time to move into meditation and explore consciousness at the next level.

Many also find themselves experiencing exhaustion which is followed by long, deep sleep intervals, sometimes lasting ten to twelve hours at a time. Please remember that your body, your being, is going through a massive change. Your vessel needs to go into the deep pause for integration, repair, and improvement. Often after a few days of extra deep sleep, one wakes up feeling the next level of amazing.

It is very important to listen deeply to what is present for you. When you are tired, you must rest. When you are feeling vital, you should move. In presence and with deep listening, you will move in harmony with your ascending being and cease moving against your natural flow. This is becoming a 5D expression in human form.

Appetite

As your body temple becomes more of a crystalline lightbody expression, the need for food shifts as well as what kinds of foods your BEing desires. Your body is waking up in frequency. This requires a next level of presence as to what you put in, on, or around your body temple. For some, food becomes less and less of a driving force. For others, as the body desires more and more, the food coming in needs to be light, pure, clean, and fresh. You are feeding the crystalline core, so what are you feeding it?

Some have also experienced a lasso effect to this, craving more and more dense foods. I believe this desire for density ties into the old imprints, patterns, and programs. It seems that along the journey of awakening, some go through both phases, an increase in density, then a sudden pivot to lighter and lighter foods that provide a lighter and lighter body response. Listen to what your body is asking for. Is it the mind asking for the old familiar, as it attempts to hold on and stay grounded in the 3D? Or, is your soul speaking through your flesh and asking to be fed with the light-bearing foods of the planet?

Memory

Ah, this one can be alarming. It has already been stated that time is collapsing and presence is the key in all things, step one. As you adjust to this level of presence, you will find that holding on to memories and what has occurred before becomes less and less available to you. Fear not, everything is alive within you. It is the mind that is releasing its hold on you. When you are optimized in presence, there is less need to retrieve what was or even project what will be. The only moment that holds any resonance is this NOW moment, this breath, as the eternal gift of presence.

Skin

This one blew me away. I have had several sacred souls report experiencing extremely dry and cracking skin of the hands, arms, and face, with most of it seemingly unresponsive to lotions, oils, or creams. After some time of this cracking and then the sloughing away of the old, they have noticed fresh new "baby" skin appearing as if overnight. This "new" skin has appeared with a light shimmer or sheen to it. The new skin seems to glisten in the light or the sun. It has a glow to it that picks up light rays and reflects them back. We are literally becoming new humans with a crystalline glow.

Heightened Senses and Sensitivities

You are most likely experiencing a massive shift in your senses and sensitivities. For the collective to rise up to the next frequency, all of your senses must not only come online, but must also become amplified at an extraordinary rate. Remember the 3D (mind) is based on separation and disconnection, while the 5D (soul feeling) is based on unification and connection.

How you arrive at the higher frequency is through your senses. They must expand exponentially to bring you home to heaven on earth and to the collective of humanity with you. This is experienced initially through light, sound, and sensation, with your smell and taste elevating over time.

Lights can be overwhelmingly bright as they are turned up. Sounds can permeate so deeply through you that they become unbearable. When all of your senses are activated at once, you may experience irritability, confusion, and even feel physically unwell. Having a controlled environment is very helpful during these times, if at all possible.

You will also notice that your empathy for people increases. You may feel what others are feeling and even begin to hear what they are thinking. At your most expanded state, words aren't really necessary, given that in 5D reality, the union is one where telepathy becomes more and more available.

Many of you started this journey highly sensitive, and as the ascension is occurring, the states of expansion can feel overwhelming at times. Be sure to take breaks from large crowds, loud people, noises, and bright lights when you become overwhelmed. It is essential to give yourself a time out by stepping outside, leaning into nature, clearing your energy, and setting your frequency. There are many tools in the next chapter for you to utilize.

Hearing and Seeing Things

As you move through this massive increase of your senses and sensitivities, the old 3D matrix has you forgetting that you are an empath, a seer, a wayshower. You are in great knowing, connected to all things through all directions and dimensions of time and space. Each human holds one or all of the "claires": clairvoyant (sight), clairsentient (feeling), clairaudient (hearing), claircognizant (clear knowing).

The "claires" will increase greatly as we ascend. Many are also seeing with their *real eyes* to *realize* what this human experience has had alive within them all along, they simply could not receive it through the 3D density lens. People are noticing shadows and figures both of light and darkness that they had not been able to see before. Light is dancing across this world with a vibrancy and lightshow display that is awe inspiring.

The Fairy

I am talking on the phone with one of my favorite deep-dive soul sisters, you know the type that goes to the core and is only really interested in the depths of life and Spirit, because who has energy for the old 3D chatter any longer, right? I am outside in the blazing hot sun of late summer. She and I are sharing the magic of creation, the joy of our breakthroughs in consciousness, and the sheer magic of being a human during this wild awakening ride. I am watering my plants with a long extending hose, and the hose becomes caught on the edge of a chair. As I turn to unwind it, a shimmer of light in fluorescent green catches my eye.

It is about two inches tall and appears to have a double set of iridescent wings, much like a dragonfly. It has a body but is in no way shaped like a dragonfly. I scream to my girlfriend, Rochelle, "Oh My Goddess! It's a Fairy!" Sheer pleasure and complete delight fills my being. I hurry to catch up with her as she flies towards a plant growing in its planter on my deck, and in that moment, poof she is gone!

Of course I imagine I am seeing things, as the programming of my four-year-old mind runs deep. But, I saw what I saw, and there is no denying it. I search through the plant and realize she had vanished. But what an absolutely magical moment!

The fairy folks are not new to me. Decades ago, while living in my magical Big Sur home, I created fairy gardens for my tiny, allusive fairy and fae friends. I grew their favorite flowers and would leave them treats of butter and sweets. In return, they would leave me gifts of smooth rocks and shiny objects that had no logical explanation as to why they would appear or how they got there. I used to make houses and fairy furniture for them. One even came to me in a lucid dream and showed me exactly how to make these treasured offerings for them.

This was, however, the first time I had seen one with my real eyes. And this, my friend, is only the beginning of such magic here on the earth plane that is awaiting for us to wake up in our fullest frequency, so we may see, hear, and receive all the splendor that is and has always been all around us.

Increased Dialogue with Self and Spirit

This one took me by surprise, and I know that I am not alone. I have literally found myself having full conversations with Spirit, my higher self, guides, and other sacred souls. I speak to them while walking throughout my day, shopping in the store, driving the car, watching a movie with my family, and on and on. The conversions come out of my heart, and the sheer increase of how often this occurs is startling.

I once asked my guides if I was losing my mind? "Yes!" they said, "YES you are, and please continue to do so. Your mind will never lead you home to the promised land of your soul's greatest expression, only your soul can guide you. Lose Your Mind, Please!"

This is the pivot point where you begin to feel the union and unity (you and I tied together) of higher dimensionality. The communion of souls, soul to self, self to Source, and soul to soul is here living and breathing through you. Yes, some may think you are losing your mind, and you can say, "Yes, I am releasing that expression to rise up to new heights."

Anxiety

Many empaths and starseeds suffer from anxiety as they navigate this earth-plane reality. You must think of your role here on planet earth as you being a master filtration system. You are not here just for your own experience but to support the collective to ascend in consciousness, and that is a multifaceted exchange. You as the filtration system means that all of the energies of this planet need to shift and respond through you and all of the others like you. Most of what you are feeling does not belong to you. Thank you for your service.

Anxiety can also be created from plugging into the matrix of fear and illusion that is being poured through the consciousness of this planet via news, social media, movies, etc. Anxiety comes from future gazing and fixating on a fear of a future scenario that will most likely never occur if you simply stop focusing upon it. Presence is the key to your peace.

Confusion

As you are moving through the process of ascension, it is very common to find yourself forgetful and confused. The mind becomes a jumble as it is releasing its programs and moving into greater presence. It is not for you to figure things "out" but to re-configure them from within. Confusion often comes from the old way of doing things which are gradually becoming unavailable to you. Everything is becoming new, and you are moving from DOing to BEing. This can feel very confusing, much like beginning to write with your non-dominant hand. It has always been there, available to you, yet it feels foreign and unfamiliar, maybe even awkward when you start adapting to using it. Take pause, breathe, find presence, and often the confusion will quickly subside. Also, there truly is no going back to the old ways of being. Find the pause and await your next divine assignment.

Isolating

You are physically, mentally, emotionally, and energetically going through A LOT. You may have a strong urge to go home, pull the blinds, and turn off your phone. That is OKAY! You are becoming a new human, and sometimes you need time to integrate all that you are experiencing. Take the space needed. Be sure, however, to not isolate to a point that you lose a grip with consciousness. We truly ride this dragon and rise up together. You are not alone!

LIGHT COUNCIL CHANNEL

"We understand, dear one, that this experience of becoming new humans is extraordinary beyond anything that you know. In fact, it is extraordinary beyond anything that any of us knows. Therefore, it is essential for you to keep reminding yourself that this is the birth of a New Earth that has never been created before, at least not in the way of which it is currently being created!

Your soul has been in preparation for this time for thousands and thousands of years, as have ours. We come to you this day for a greater knowing to be remembered through you. We are hearing from you that it feels as if parts of your inner world are dying, and indeed we say that this is an accurate expression. The old of the inner and the outer must die, fall away, and transmute to allow the new crystalline expression of your soul's truth to shine freely through.

Worry not. This is divine, and you are not alone.

There are tools and support for you with each breath. If at any moment you feel as if it is all too much, then find a place of surrender. We know this is a conflict to what you are used to from your 3D lens. Your familiarity is to power through, to move through the density, and scramble about as a solo flier who is solving the problem and foraging a new path. In this new frequency, dear one, you surrender it all over to higher self and Source, and in that very moment, in that exact second, all has been sorted, handled, and aligned for you. This is the potency of you as a creator in your fully expressed, authentically true state of sovereignty.

It is here for you. We love you dearly, and we are here by your side in each moment, remembering you and championing you on to your greatest New-Earth expression."

- The Light Council

Chapter Thirteen
Ascension Tools

"There's always another level up. There's always another ascension.
More grace, more light, more generosity, more compassion,
more to shed, more to grow."

~ Elizabeth Gilbert

Yes, the list of ascension symptoms is extensive but so is the offering of tools available for you to support your precious self through this very intense journey. Worry not. As The Light Council has assured me, there are many tools available to navigate through this wild ride. These tools are also incredibly useful for keeping you on pulse, moving ahead in your abundant life feeling present and centered, and for finding your phenomenal.

All of the tools are useful. Try picking one or two at a time and really embracing each to the point of familiarity, embodiment, and mastery. If you slowly integrate the tools, you will be able to track which one has the greatest effect. It is also noteworthy to remember that you are a living, breathing organism in a massive transformation portal, and what works for a week or two may not work in the same way the following week. This is not a one-size-fits-all kind of rise. You are shifting so rapidly that it is important to bring in all of the tools. Just like a carpenter building a house, you need more than just a hammer and a saw. You need an entire set of tools to navigate your way through to the beautiful, fully constructed home of your heart's greatest expression.

The following tools are for you to practice and implement into daily ritual. Some are quick and easy, and you may find yourself needing to go to them several times a day. Play with them to see what works for you at any given moment, which ones you would like to expand upon, and which ones may not be for you at this time. Make them your own. You are a creator and unique through and through.

Breath

Pranayama is the practice of unifying the vital lifeforce energy of breath. The beauty of this tool is that it is always accessible to you, anytime, anywhere. There are several different breathing techniques to support the ascension journey. Again, this is not a one-size-fits-all approach, and you are forever changing, so play, practice, and see what is true for you.

The first step is simply finding your breath. Close your eyes and connect to the breath. Explore with it and see where it takes you and where in your body it does not. Invite it to explore every corner. Even this simple exercise can have profound effects upon your being. Your breath brings you into presence, creates a pause, and calms the mind. It moves you out of your mind and into your body, bringing you home.

Next is one of the simplest yet most profound of all of the tools. Take in a regular breath and massively slow down the outbreath. See if you can double the length of time it takes to exhale from a regular inhalation. This works by physiologically shifting your body from the sympathetic nervous system, fight or flight response, to the parasympathetic, rest and digest response. This breathing tool calms down your central nervous system and is the key to presence, allowing you to focus.

Box Breathing

The box breathing technique is said to be used by the Navy SEALs, as it heightens performance, stamina, and focus. It is breathing in a rhythmic count, such as breathing in for five seconds, holding your breath at the top for five seconds, breathing out for five seconds, and holding the out breath at the bottom for five seconds. A few rounds of this technique will bring you into presence and laser focus.

There are many pranayama practices as well as much art and science dedicated to the breath. It is your first gift both given and received upon entry into this human existence as well as your last offering upon completion. It is also here with you in every moment to nourish, ground, and exchange with you and mother earth.

There are many styles and types of breathwork practices. I highly suggest finding a well-trained breathwork facilitator and diving into the profound well of deep healing that this ancient practice has to offer you.

Meditation

It has been said that prayer is speaking to God and meditation is listening. Meditation has been around forever, but perhaps it has never been more necessary than it is right now. Finding the still point within, quieting the mind to shift from the 3D mind to the 5D soul expression, really, truly is one of the fundamental, necessary steps to transform and rise up, making meditation an essential tool in your toolbox. It is important to understand that there is not one way to meditate.

In the current world, with everything moving so quickly, and with so much stimulation, a human's average attention span, according to a study done by Microsoft in 2018, was, wait for it, take a breath in, yup, that was it, only eight seconds!

According to the National Science Foundation, an average person has about twelve to sixty thousand thoughts per day. Of those thoughts, 80% are negative, and 95% are repetitive loops. It is seemingly quite the challenge to find the full zen of the void of total silence these days, is it not? Finding that pause button takes practice and consistency just like every mastered skill.

I highly suggest in the beginning to hand over the idea that you are going to sit and meditate for thirty minutes, immediately clear your mind, find the zero point, and experience nirvana. That is a great intention, but what usually happens is a thousand things run through your brain, each one seemingly more important than the last: Was that my phone? I have to pee. That noise is bugging me. I am uncomfortable in this shirt. I forgot that email. I am cold. I am hot. I am hungry. I forgot to call Gail. My face itches. And on, and on. All of it happens.

Let's walk into the process with an intention to see what is possible, while seeking for presence, patience, commitment, and ease. Start with a few minutes and grow from there. If you added just one minute a day in under a month, you would have twenty to thirty minutes of peace and alignment.

Find your favorite spot, make sure it is distraction free, and sit in any fashion that feels good. You do not have to be in a full lotus position, on a meditation pillow, with incense burning and eleven white candles lit, unless that brings you comfort, bliss, and joy. Meditation, like most tools, does not require a lot of outside things. It is an inside game, so play with it.

Sit down, get comfortable, close your eyes, and listen. Listen to all of the chatter for a few seconds, then invite your mind to focus on your breath. The mind loves a job, your breath is now the mind's job. Try following your breath down through your body, out the first or root chakra (tip of the tailbone), and go all the way to the center of the earth to see what you find there. Swim in the waters of the crystalline core. See if you find your core crystal, which is your soul's marker, to connect to the earth plane. Next, see if you can find your soul's name written on that crystal. This in itself could be your five-minute meditation.

Next, allow your breath to move up through the same portal that it had descended through. Come back up through all of your chakras and out the top of your head or crown chakra. Journey to the grand central sun or to your "star system," should you be familiar with the one your starseed soul has originated from. Explore what that feels like. What do you see? What do you remember? Then loop back down to your heart. From here you should notice that you are calmer and more present. It may take you days or weeks to familiarize yourself with this part of the journey alone.

Meditation is also not a one-size-fits-all expression. You have to find your natural exploration. Some enjoy following along to guided meditations. Find my meditation store link below, it is an excellent way to get started. I do suggest, however, playing with what you have learned in your guided meditation to center yourself or simply listening to one to get into the zone and then turning it off to explore what you find on your own. The meditative state is where higher consciousness, God, creator, and higher beings find the space to commune and communicate with you. Remember, prayer is speaking to God, meditation is listening. Create the space within your meditation for listening to receive your truest guidance.

To access my meditation store, please scan this QR code.

Prayer

Speaking to God, or your higher self, brings you into greater connection. This supports you in gaining clarity about what it is that you are actually willing to experience as well as in creating an affirmation of your willingness to receive that which you most desire.

Prayer is personal, and it can look any way you choose, much like meditation. Prayer can be gratitude, acknowledging all of the things that are working so beautifully in your life in a way that anchors them through your heart's expression of thanks. Where there is gratitude, there is abundance.

Prayer can be a mantra, a song, a poem, or the truth of what it is that you are willing to experience. It is best to always ask with the intention of how you are willing to "feel" in response to the thing or things that you are asking to receive or experience. I often request, "By receiving this, I ask to feel in a state higher than the one I am currently experiencing."

It is essential to never limit what you ask of the Universe. You could ask for a million dollars, but what if there were ten million awaiting you? You would never want to limit the infinite abundance of divine Source. You could instead ask for the freedom of abundance that is available for you to feel free, or relaxed, or sourced, or all of it really. Ask for this or greater.

Prayer is your communion or communication that goes beyond the mind and connects you into the deep well of infinite possibilities. Don't wait until you are in a crisis. Instead get in the habit of your daily exchange with Source and watch your life change each day.

Earthing in Nature

Get your feet to the earth! This concept is an ancient practice that lost its mojo when we started wearing soled shoes, thus disconnecting us from our natural exchange with the earth's energy. Everything is energy. You are a vibrating being who runs energy through each cell of your body, and everything is frequency that responds to that energy.

The earth holds electromagnetic frequency as well. By design, you as a human exchange energy with the earth. The Light Council showed me that for the higher realms of energy to be received by mother earth, it first needs to flow through your body to be received by the earth. You are the conduit to transform Mother Gaia into her highest frequency. There is no separation between you, the earth, the rocks, the trees, and every other living thing that is here with you in this earth dance. The frequency goes both ways.

To earth, you simply place your bare feet or entire body upon Mother Gaia. This grounds you. You are pure energy expressing itself through flesh and bone. When you come to the earth, she offers to ground your energy through her. She smiles up at you in gratitude for this ever-expanding exchange.

Your home has electricity running through it. In order for this to happen, your home is wired with copper to ground the frequency into the earth. If your home did not have this feature, too much electricity would run through and ignite fire. Your body is the same. You must ground your energy through the earth in order to balance your own energy flow.

It is simple, and the simplest of practices are far too often forgotten or left behind. If you are feeling anxiety, energetically off, confused, or overly stimulated, get to the earth ASAP. Exchange your energy with hers and feel the instant transformation, as calm and ease instantly moves through you.

Make it a daily practice to sustain and maintain your energy body and to fulfill your agreements here with Mother Gaia. Lay your back upon her lush bounty and let her hold you. It is all she has ever wanted, to hold you like a mother. Gaze up at the sky and allow the light of the sun to shine through you, activating the higher light codes living within your DNA, then exchange this light with the earth. This practice is like offloading the battery storage of old energy so that new, more potent energy can move through you.

If you are not in a place that allows for you to find the earth easily, then do so in your mind's eye and feel the exchange. There are also grounding pads you can purchase and plug into the grounding port of your electric outlets, which help to support this energy exchange. This practice has been known to reduce the inflammation in your physical body, shift your mood, and even lessen chronic pain.

Pineal Gland Activation

Sitting with your face to the sun, specifically your third eye, supports the cellular activation of the pineal gland. The pineal gland is considered to be the source of your intuitive knowledge. It is your lightbody's communication with your physical being.

Sungazing has been in practice for thousands of years. Traditionally it is done at dusk or dawn with eyes squinted and barely open. This can be very intense for your eyes, especially with the intensity of the sun in current times. Your eyes do not need to be open to receive the full benefits.

It only takes five to ten minutes daily to receive the recharge from the sun's light. It occurs even through the clouds, so do not worry if you live in an environment that does not give you the pure light of daily sun. Gazing at the moon or the stars will also have an effect upon your pineal gland by activating your galactic remembrance and supporting your being through the ascension process.

Water! In, On, and Around You!

The element of water is your greatest friend. Your body is a mirror to earth, and she is made up of 70-80% water, just as you are. Water is the conduit of electricity, of frequency. If there is a lack of water within your being, your electromagnetic frequency is not able to conduct energy freely through your earth vessel.

Water purifies by clearing toxins and other waste products from your body. When you are in a state of activating your energy body, or creating any changes on a cellular level, water must be present to assist the process. It is recommended, as a minimum, to drink at least half of your body weight in ounces of water each day. Water can ground you and allow for greater flow through your connective tissue as well as your life. It amplifies your greatest lifeforce energy or chi.

Get water in, on, and around your body often. A trip to the beach, lake, or river can do wonders for your spirits. A jump in the water will clear negative energies from your being. The air near the ocean holds negative ions which also serve to lift your mood and lighten your spirits. Floating in water brings you back the remembrance of the womb, an environment perfectly regulated to serve you, as you were safe, held, nourished, rocked, and loved.

Water is an endless loop on planet earth. The rain falls and gathers in ponds, rivers, and pools. The water nourishes the plants. The plants turn it into fuel, then into gas which is released back to the atmosphere. Water then falls back to earth as rain, fog, or dew. The bodies of water gather the water. Then through the heat of the sun, evaporation occurs, offering the water back into the atmosphere. The cycle is an endless, closed loop of exchange.

With this understanding, you could gain the awareness that the sip of water you are about to drink has your ancestors' tears within it. Just as with all things, you are eternally connected to all time and space through each droplet of water.

Washing with Water

Jesus washed the feet of his disciples to honor the truth that we are eternally connected through the waters. Water was and is still used in ceremony and purification and as an act of anointment and honor. Baptism occurs in water. Rosewater placed upon your third eye is an act of holy communion. Water is powerful.

Washing your hair is another powerful tool for clearing your physical and energetic body. This is my go-to when I am feeling distorted or off pulse. Your hair holds memory, and it operates like an antenna. It gathers all of the energy that is present around you. Hair tests can even show what you have ingested into your physical body months or even years after the fact. Hair is also the cosmic connector.

Many religions suggest that their followers do not cut their hair so that they may hold on to their power and memories. The biblical story of Samson tells the tale of his power being lost when his hair was cut. During World War II, the United States brought the natives into combat because of their amazing ability to track the enemy's location. Once the native people were initiated into the Army, the next step was to cut their hair in accordance with military standards. Their tracking abilities diminished greatly, if not entirely, after their hair was cut.

To sustain and manage your energy body at the highest level, be mindful to wash your hair more frequently. This is most important after you have been engaging in large crowds of people or when you are going through a particularly large ascension surge. The instant energy shift that this simple ritual provides is truly amazing. In my household, my family at times will say, "Hey, do you need to wash your hair?" when they see that I am not operating as my highest self. Sometimes we need reminders, and each time I heed their wisdom, I am grateful for the shift in my own energy.

Clearing Energies and Bringing Your Parts Home

Energy clearing is an absolute must and essential to sustaining and maintaining your well-being while navigating through this awakening journey. You wash your homes, cars, clothes, and physical bodies, yet the energy body is often left unacknowledged. There are many ways to do this. What is most important is that you are actually doing it. As you walk through your day engaging with the world, you are also exchanging energy with everyone and everything. You are connected to it all.

Each time you cast a gaze or a thought towards another human, whether it be positive or negative, you have chorded with him or her energetically. Being in the presence of another, an exchange occurs, and pieces of the other human are magnetized and become attached to you. This experience, from an energetic perspective, is like a mesh of energy lightbeams shooting strings of light to everyone, all the time. It is a huge web of connections.

As you are awakening and becoming more and more sensitive to your empathic truth, this becomes more and more obvious, maybe even more and more uncomfortable. I suggest setting intentions of clearing your energy body whenever you are feeling distorted. The moment you feel your energy drop, when a wave of sadness or frustration runs over you for no apparent reason, or when your thoughts turn away from the positive, it is your indication that it is time to do an energy clearing.

Begin with closing your eyes and taking three deep breaths. Ask Archangel Michael to come on your behalf. Begin to envision liquid light pouring down from heaven through the crown of your head, filling every cell of your body, then flowing out through the tip of your tailbone, the souls of your feet, and each finger tip. Begin to see this pure crystalline light energy streaming through the front and back of each chakra. See the light begin to pour over the entirety of your physical body, into your auric field, and possibly into the space of which you are currently residing. Breath the light through and say, "I release all that no longer serves my highest and greatest good. I cut all chords and all attachments. I send everything and everyone that is complete for me to the light."

This can be done anywhere and at any time, even at the dinner table. No one needs to know. It is a beautiful practice to perform this clearing in the actual shower as water is pouring over you. Some of the greatest clearings and holy communions with your higher self and Source occur in the shower!

After you clear, it is hugely supportive to welcome your fragmented pieces back to you. We as souls often fragment or fractal parts of ourselves. You are most likely familiar with more extreme cases such as dissociative identity disorder, formerly known as multiple personality disorder. The mind and the soul will split or fragment to protect at times. Simply say, "I call back all of my parts, fragmented or otherwise, washed in light, and fully and completely reassembled into myself for wholeness, fullness, and completeness." This is beautifully incorporated at the end of a clearing.

As with all things, gratitude is the attitude. Complete your clearing and re-claiming by expressing, "Thank you, thank you, thank you. It is done!"

Energy Protection

You wear a down jacket when it is cold, long sleeves when the sun is pouring on your skin for an extended time, gloves while pruning roses, glasses to shield the sun, but the energy body is often left to fend for itself out there.

Energy protection is paired well with clearing your energy body and is just as important. After you have done your clearing, before you go out into the world or even get on a Zoom or phone call, it is wise to put on your energy body protection. There are several ways to do this. It is best to find what works for you and change it up from time to time, thus allowing you to stay active, attentive, and alert.

The "Light Bubble" method is probably the most familiar. Simply envision a beautiful bubble of light forming in your heart. Envision this gem of light as it begins growing through every cell of your body until it encompasses the entirety of your auric field and beyond, usually two to three feet beyond your body. Pick a color that feels good. I suggest white or gold, as they are higher-vibrational colors, but trust your intuition. It is a beautiful practice to wrap and seal your bubble of light with a pink energy, as this allows for the pure exchange of love to be given and received.

You may even envision yourself jumping into a glowing, electric, light-filled, hazmat-style suit and then simply saying "Zip Up!" as you move out into the world. It does not matter what you choose as your protection. It is most important, however, that you are protecting yourself at every turn.

Moving the Body

Your body is becoming crystalline. It is the biggest shift through density that our physical expressions have ever encountered. Your body needs you to MOVE so that the energy held within your cells may be free. The carbon coding of your body is attempting to break itself free; it does that through expression and movement. Yoga, dance, hiking, walking, sweating, jumping, vibrating, rolling, swimming, and even having sex are all great ways to free the body of some of its density. It must be done daily, so pick your favorite activities and get moving!

Mind Reprogramming

This is perhaps the most complexicated of all of the tools. The MIND! If you want things to be different, you need to become different and think differently. Your brain holds the programming of thoughts often handed to you by outside forces, begining with your parents who received their programming from their parents, and on down the line it goes. Your mind is like a sponge absorbing it all, especially during childhood.

There are societal programs that have been held in mass conscious-ness as well. It is arduous to begin the reprogramming because you don't know what you don't know, and mostly the mind doesn't know its programmed or wired for certain thoughts. The first step is to identify that perhaps there is another way and to then change your mind.

What you think creates your reality. This you know.

Everytime you think a thought that doesn't feel good, you get to take a two to three second pause and call back that thought, change it, and cast the spell to something new. The first step is simply observing your thoughts and beginning to decipher which thoughts are serving you and which are not. This involves just observing, not judging.

After some self-observation, you could grab a stretchy bracelet of some sort, something comfortable that is easy on and easy off. Begin with it on your left wrist, and each time you think a thought that doesn't feel good, take off the bracelet, correct the thought to something positive, and put the bracelet on the right wrist. Each time you catch a thought, you will go through this process, left to right, right to left, to support embodying the conscious-brain repatterning. The first few days you will change your bracelet often, and within three days, you will be amazed by how differently you are thinking and feeling.

Chapter Fourteen
Abracadabra

The magic of words is that they have power to do more than convey meaning; not only do they have the power to make things clear, they make things happen.

~ Frederick Buechner

Words are powerful; they hold frequency and vibration. This is the energy of all creation. The Light Council often says, "Words do not teach, but they serve as a directive of frequency that you as humans have become accustomed to understanding as one means of communion or communication." You have noticed through this transmission that I love to play with words. Indeed it is true, as the play of words has significant power. As you continue to evolve in higher and higher frequencies, you will find a natural shift to using fewer and fewer words. This is because words in many ways were created from the 3D lens, and as we rise, we are remembered into the greater expression of frequency which happens through thought. In time, we will be more and more available to communicate telepathically, through thought or through pure frequency. We already do it all the time. You know like when the phone rings and you say, "OMGoddess! I was just thinking about you." It is like that, minus the ringing phone and more in a full-hearted resonance of that which the other soul is wanting to share, but that is an entire book in itself. Oh, the places we shall go.

So, words hold power because they hold vibration and because we have attached certain meanings to them through our 3D lens. Many believe, and I agree, that certain words have been empowered greatly to keep others oppressed and in pain. We can see, however, that the "oppressed" use these words to actually empower themselves, hence shifting the power of the word. There is a C word and an N word that comes to mind, and honestly I'll leave it at that because I choose not to battle with either of them.

Words are powerFULL. Abracadabra is a Hebrew word that literally translates into "It will be created in my word," or "As I speak it, so shall it be," basically "Your word is your wand." Your words hold power, and with a few shakes of your wand, many of them can be transformed to expand frequency and empower you. I believe there are several words or phrases in the English language that are ready to transform, and as we transform them, it feels like a tool we can use to get a different command upon them, giving us an opportunity to start using them to serve our expansion rather than limitation.

Should/Could/Can

Are you "shoulding" all over yourself and others? The word "should" holds a frequency of shame and judgment. It does not feel good to say it, does it? It feels like a burden, an obligation, an expectation. Most of us are programmed from early on to "should." You are told "you should" by parents, adults, teachers, mentors, coaches, and leaders that you admire and look to for guidance.

The second I tell you, "Hey you! You know what? You really should stop suffering and do all of the things already," I am shaming you and overriding your sovereignty. When we stop "shoulding" all over ourselves and each other, then perhaps we will be more equipped to listen to the truth of the calling of our own souls, our inner wisdom, and start making choices that align with us and with our purpose here on planet earth.

So how do we do this? We move to the word "could." "Hey you! You know what? You really *could* choose to stop suffering and move towards doing the things that you love." Do you feel the difference in this? It doesn't hold judgment but rather a belief in the other. It serves as an inspiration to them. The word "could" honors that each being, especially yourself, is sovereign and gets to choose over and over again what is for them. It turns from a conclusion into a curiosity.

Try it on for yourself by saying, "I *should* XYZ." Now take a moment to feel that statement, really feel it. What do you notice? Now try saying, "I *could* XYZ!" How does that feel? Notice if one is lighter in the body than the other? It's all frequency.

When you are "coulding," you are moving into curiosity. Could I? The moment you move from a conclusion to a question, the Universe and all of its splendor comes pouring forth in excitement to show you what indeed IS possible for YOU. "Shoulds" fall hard and flat. "Coulds" lift an eye up in the realm of possibility. Feel the rise in energy?

This brings us to the word "can." Ah, the power of CAN. It is courageous. It is empowering. It is a proclamation of ownership, and this frequency is the frequency that creates worlds. I Can and I AM! When this proclamation is brought to the forefront of your body, mind, and soul, there is a magnificent synergy where all of consciousness comes to your beckoning. I can call, and magic occurs. Feel it?

So "should" holds you in a frequency of shame, judgment, and "not enoughness." "Could" is "curious" and opens the door of deeper inquiry into what is possible and what is desired in actuality. "Can" becomes the fierce proclamation of courage and power and brings all into universal order to match your absolute truth. Please remember that in each moment you are choosing. You choose with your mind, heart, and soul, and your words become a match to that vibration. As you release the programs of the old limitations and move more freely into your sovereignty, leave no stone unturned. Your word is your wand!

Trying

"You must unlearn what you have learned.
Try not. Do or do not. There is no try."

~ Yoda, The Empire Strikes Back

A truly lackluster word is the word "try." It holds about as much conviction in your vibrational state as a feather blowing in the wind. When you move from the space of "I will try," you are affirming to the cells of your body and the elasticity of your mind that this thing holds very little priority within you.

When you are in a proclamation of "I will try" or "I am trying," you are telling the Universe and your own inner systems that this thing which you are "trying for" basically has already won, or rather you have already surrendered over to it and are defeated in some ways.

It is in the moment when you proclaim I AM with conviction that the things become one with you. Remember, everything is frequency. I AM healed. I AM financially free. I Am done. I Am ready.

Whatever it may be for you, the powerplay, because you are a powerful and infinite being, comes with the I AM proclamation. This puts "trying" not just behind you but in another arena all together. No more trying, you are becoming, you ARE. When you proclaim that all of the cells of your body respond to the frequency that proclaiming allows for, it is in that very moment when everything within and around you changes. I AM free. So it is. So it shall be. Claim it Sister!

Work

I, in full truth, consider "work" to be a four letter word. Not that I am not willing to show up and put in my essence for creation, but we really need to stop working on everything. You have heard it a hundred times. You have probably said it a million times. I am going to have to work on that. I can hear you right now saying, "I am going to work on releasing *try* and *should* from my vocabulary." You have done enough work on yourself. You have done enough work on your relationships, on your goals, on your health. Work feels heavy, does it not? What if you were to move beyond "working" on yourself or things into a space of allowing for the resolve or experience you desire to rise up within you?

Do you feel the difference? When you move into a state of allowance, you are indeed stepping into your greatest, most sovereign, and truest expression of yourself. At that moment, the healing is already in full motion. "Working on it" and "trying to" resonate similarly in the body. Trying implies a lack of belief or agreement to getting there. While working on it implies that it will be arduous, take time, and most likely be hard. Aren't you tired of all of that hard work?

From the lens of dimensional shifting, in 3D, you work on things because you are vibrating in that lower density of lack, fear, scarcity, and ultimately separation. From a 5D lens, you know that you are, in fact, one with everything and everyone. There is no scarcity or separation from this lens, therefore, there is nothing to work on and everything to become one with. All you must do is allow it to be part of your daily experience. You truly can have, be, live, create, and experience anything you can imagine. You are that powerful, and from this place, it is not through effort that it is made so but rather through you remembering, claiming, and becoming. Now that is a whole lot more fun than working on it, is it not?

I Am Sorry/ Ho'oponopono

Ah, the magical three words "I am sorry" can be so incredibly healing for someone to receive when they are hurting: *I am so sorry for your loss. I am sorry I hurt your feelings.* Sorry by definition means feeling sorrow, sympathy, regret, or penitence. What a beautiful offering of love.

And here is the thing with sorry, it is used so much for everything that when it can truly have its greatest impact, the sentiment is so often lost because of the myriad of less appropriate ways it is used outside of special circumstances.

Many say "I am sorry" for everything: *I am sorry you stepped on my foot. I'm sorry that I'm standing next to you because maybe I'm in your way.* Sorry has become a staple in most human expressions and especially those of women, so much so that once you fine-tune your hearing to this word, you will begin to feel that it has become, in many ways, an apology for existence.

The opportunity at hand is, as it is in most things, to become very discerning about the usage of sorry. Could you say "thank you" more than "I am sorry"? *Thank you for your patience* instead of *Sorry I am late. Thank you for honoring one more question and giving me a little more of your time.*

It is time that we stop apologizing for presence, accidents, and situations beyond our control. Once you begin to pay attention to how often "I am sorry" is used to compress one's presence or energy, you will find a natural desire to use the word very differently, perhaps in a way that empowers and strengthens.

The Ho'oponopono Prayer is very popular for good reason. It is a beautiful Hawaiian prayer that many have found both comfort and healing in: "I am sorry, please forgive me, thank you, I love you." I have been playing with my own version of it as of late: "Thank you, I love you, I stand in forgiveness with you." This feels lighter in my being, unless of course there is a genuine need for apology.

Remember please that words are vibration. It has less to do with the words themselves and more to do with the imprint of the words upon you and how they make you feel. Again, as with all things, you first need a strong conviction in your presence in every moment to be feeling your way through words. The tendency is to go unconscious and parrot the words you have heard forever without the awareness of the pain and limitations they may be creating within you.

LIGHT COUNCIL CHANNEL

"Dear ones, we come with an urgent message for you this day. It is not merely that it will be nice or more pleasant for you when you raise your vibrational frequency. It is a matter of urgency. We are summoning you from the powers that be from high above and deep within. We summon you this day and the days to follow to be mindful of all your intentional thoughts, of all your expressed words, and of all the ways you are sustaining, maintaining, and elevating your frequencies in any given moment.

All of your thoughts, words, and frequencies are to be in service to the outcome of the collective's energy, as it is in an expansion mode that is beyond explanation. The challenge upon you now is the colliding of worlds from an old frequency that cannot be sustained and maintained in the light of the new frequency. It is as if these two worlds are standing head to head, eye to eye, nose to nose, breath to breath.

The forces of limitation and contraction are in such a high elevation of fear that they cannot yet put down their weapons of distancing and separation. They believe that their fundamental wellbeing is dependent upon them being in resistance to the allowing of what their souls are desiring to actually move through them.

You are to lay down your shields. You are to bestow love as the frequency that you now have greater access to, but yet may still feel unfamiliar with. Your shining light of love is the only thing that will support the breakdown and therefore the transformation from the attachment of fear itself. We do not say this in a light manner.

We are speaking to this as the vibrational frequency. It is the frequency that your state of acceptance, of honor, and of love holds. When you meet anger with the energy of fear or fear with energy of anger, you are only pouring fuel upon its fire. We understand that this is counterintuitive to what it is that you have been programmed to know. We will remind you that there is a wisdom that is available within the essence of your souls that in fact does resonate and does understand how this must be."

– The Light Council

Chapter Fifteen
The Power of the Word

"Words have energy and power with the ability to help, to heal, to hinder, to hurt, to harm, to humiliate, and to humble."

~ Yehuda Berg

Sacred Fuck YES

There is an amazing flow of divine Source that pours through you when you find and honor your Sacred Fuck Yes! It is potent beyond pretty much anything other than the Sacred Hell No, but we will get to that later. Yes. It is a full sentence that can add significant juice, flair, and unexpected magic to your daily flow. Yes aligns the Universe to bring you to the things that you most want and the things that you most want to you in a harmonious and ease-filled way. Yes holds a power and an activation in its frequency that few other words hold.

Yes can be rich and deep medicine for you, especially if you tend to hold back from having new experiences out of fear. Yes, Yes, Yes! Play with it in your mouth. Say it out loud with different tones. How does it roll off of your tongue? How does it light up your soul? More life-changing moments, significant adventures, and divine synchronicities have occurred through this word than probably any other word.

Have you ever taken a Thirty-Day Say Yes Challenge? For thirty days say Yes to everything that is offered, unless, of course, it goes against your moral compass or simply is not a good thing. Say Yes where you feel that edge of contraction, where the fear, otherwise known as excitement, rises up in your belly. Everything you want, precious soul, is usually living just outside of your comfort zone. Sometimes you have to stretch your web, contort the matrix, stretch your essence, step up and step out, color outside of the lines, and say Yes to see what awaits you.

I heard a story once of a woman who took the Thirty-Day Say Yes Challenge. She was invited to a dinner party that she really didn't feel like attending, as it was midweek, it was a further commute than she liked, it was late, she was tired, the moon was squaring mars, you know, all the things. But, she had agreed to say Yes in order to stretch and see what was possible. She went and met the man who ended up becoming her husband. The Yes is powerful indeed.

There is the Sacred Yes and the Sacred Fuck Yes, and they hold different frequencies. The first may activate a sensation in your body like a joyful, curious flutter. The latter is more like a tsunami of full-body transmission, often resulting in truth bumps rolling from your head to your toes. It is important to feel the difference, as the Sacred Fuck Yes is often fabulously aligned within you for something pretty massive to enter into your field to change your life.

It has been stated, and I wholeheartedly agree, that if it is not a Yes, then it is a No. The body knows, the body is your pendulum of truth, it holds all of your answers, all of them, and it knows them within the first twenty seconds, probably the first two.

Another amazing opportunity for you to feel your way forward through divine inspiration is when you move out of the programmed mind matrix and into the authentic feeling of self-actualized truth.

It is so much easier to find soul answers to your questions from the feeling state. The mind plays games of figuring it out, while the body figures it in, showing you alignment through frequency. The first answer your body gives you is the correct answer. Oh My Goddess, the hours that could be saved from tormenting over what decision to make by realizing the answer is there all along, from the first two to twenty seconds a question is asked. A Maybe is a No, and Yes stands alone like a perfectly poised ballerina, front and center stage, gracing the entire space.

Your body holds all of the wisdom. It is your pendulum. How you access this wisdom is through your presence and your deep listening. When the body feels a Yes, it rises up with excitement, like a rapid inhale that lifts your chest, like a gasp of air. You know this feeling when something amazing happens and you gasp with pleasure. The Yes is always a lift up in your vibrational frequency. The No feels like an exhale in your body, your body compresses and goes a bit flat.

The physical cue matches the level of the experience. If it is an all-expense-paid trip to Australia and that excites you, it may feel profound in your body. Whereas, if you have just been given a scratch ticket, it might be less noticeable. The key is to feel your way through. The smaller the thing, the more subtle the body's response. This is why it is so important to be in presence and practice with things that are inconsequential, such as: *Do I drink mint tea or peach tea? Do I take this supplement today or not?* Once you have practiced some on this level, you can begin experimenting with the big, life-changing questions.

Play with this in everything and begin to fine-tune your body's response to truth within your physical vessel. This is such a powerful tool because it is always accessible to you and you need nothing outside of yourself to bring forth clarity. Play with this with things you already know that you love or that you know that you don't. Then observe your body's response. Ask your body everything. Fine-tune your body's pendulum; it will take you far in active decision making with confidence and greater ease.

Learning the sacred Yes is not everyone's medicine. Sometimes the greatest opportunity and strongest empowered move is in saying No. This is where your personal inventory comes into practice. Do you say Yes out of true resonance, desire, and body alignment? Or have you been programmed to say Yes to make others happy, to prove your worth, or out of fear of disappointing another? This is a very potent pivot point and requires rawthentic truth and a strong determination to rise up to a new, empowered state to honor your sacred No.

It is not uncommon to find this humming through women more than men, I have found. It is that very outdated program of being the "good girl," saying Yes, and making sure that everyone is happy, except yourself, of course. You cannot say enough Yeses in a single lifetime to make up for a void of your own worth. You can try, as many have, and you will feel run down, suffer from anxiety, say sorry most of the time, have little freedom of time, and eventually feel resentful, that is if your body does not break down first. Yes and worth are not an even exchange, my friend.

If Yes is your go-to, then guess what? There is a soulution, the Hell No!

The Power of NO

NO! Oh my, this one is the other powerhouse on the playground. Like salt and pepper, Yes and No have very different flavors, and each play their own role, complimenting each other greatly.

No, No, NO! Bring on your inner two-year-old self and let him or her shine in true power. No, No, No! If it is your super human power to embody and embrace the Hell No, then let's go.

No is a complete sentence. Breathe that in, as I kNOw this is not the first time you've heard these words, but have you received them fully? No does not need to be followed by any explanation of why, an excuse, a story, or a negotiation of something else that you could say Yes to later. No is No. Or, you could say No, Thank You, as that is kind and even more complete.

The further along your walk is on this creatrix, this ever-expanding life journey of consciousness, the more you will find the need for you to say No is. In truth, the more you listen to your truest awakened self, and move from that place of alignment, and become the divine creator of your reality, the more things you will need to say No to. This is not because these things are wrong or bad or because you're practicing no longer saying Yes out of guilt or obligation, but it is due to the sheer volume of what is coming towards you.

You will need to find your No and use it sometimes for things you would really like to say Yes to and truly enjoy. As you are experiencing sourced, awakened living more and more, the Universe begins to flow through you more grandly and rapidly. You will have to say No sometimes simply to allow for all of the magic to flow freely through.

What is most important here is discernment and getting clear on your true "why." This is where the lens turns into the mirror that you get to take a long look into and get very clear as to the truth of where you are at in current time. Do a deep self-assessment dive and personal inventory. When you get real with yourself, then and only then can you make a decision to try on the other frequency for some time and heal the wound that kept you locked in one frequency or another in the first place.

Here are a few questions to ask yourself:

- Do I say Yes to things I know I do not want to do?

- Do I say Yes to please others instead of myself?

- Do I resent my Yes later?

- Do I say Yes more than No?

- Do I say No because I am afraid to have the experience?

- Do I say No because of a belief of limitation of time, money, or love?

- Do I regret it when I say No most of the time?

- Do I say No more than I say Yes?

After getting really, really clear about what is true for you, one way to play in shifting this frequency is to begin playing with the other frequency and seeing how it feels. After all, it is all an experiment. Take on the Thirty-Day Yes or No Challenge, depending on what you most need, and see what comes up for you. The Thirty-Day No Challenge asks you to pause, feel all the way into what is true for you before immediately saying Yes. Listen for your body's response. Perhaps you might say, "Let me get back to you in an hour," and truly feel your way through.

When I, as a recovering "Yeser," started shifting this into greater discernment, things started rapidly becoming clearer and clearer. The power of moving away from the "shoulding" of the mind into the clarity and the truth of the soul is a massively potent shift in consciousness and has great effect in every expression of your already amazing life.

The space between the Yes and the No is an interesting opportunity for empaths. This is different from moving from programs of lack or limitation. The truth is that sensitive souls can make the greatest of plans weeks in advance, and as the day rolls around, they can feel a huge dip in resonance and truly no longer feel alignment. This can be a challenge and often disappoints many hearts along the way.

There are subtleties of the Fuck Yes and the Hmm, Yes (feels good but not in full frequency). The full-body Fuck Yes means this thing is for you. The Hmm, Yes is to be felt through, perhaps explored a bit further. Personally, when feeling the curiosity of the Hmm, Yes, I now say, "I will have to let you know as the day gets closer, as I'm not yet clear." I also offer, "If you need to know right now, then the answer is No. If I can feel my way through with spaciousness, I will then let you know as we get closer." I then ask, "By when would you need to know?"

This is living in the "and" and not the "or" and has saved me many times of doing things I didn't feel connected to as it approached. It provides us all an amazing opportunity to fine-tune to the next level of deep truth and soul wisdom that lives within our cells.

Play with it all. Find your Yes if it stretches you to the next level of experiences and possibilities. Find your No if boundaries and worth are being offered up as the pivot point for transformation at this time. Find your "let me get back to you" as the stepping stone to greater empowerment, allowing you to take pause for clarity and alignment. You know what you know, and when something is right and alive within you, every part of your body will sing with delight and excitement.

The key to it all is that once you have decided, then it is done! Stand in the choice and let it be complete. There is no freedom in second guessing. Trust your inner wisdom, feel your way through because the next Fuck Yes opportunity is coming right around the corner. You will then be ready to receive it with your full-body Yes!

Words That Create
I AM

The words "I AM" are the absolute strongest proclamation of your truth, sovereignty, and power and are perhaps the most potent conviction you can summon forth. As you speak "I AM," it is in that very moment when you stand steady, fast, and true, so unwavering in your proclamation, that every cell of your body, every tendril of frequency, and the entire Universe at large beacons and bows to receive that which you are proclaiming. There is no stronger truth in all of the Universe.

I AM is the frequency of being that which you are becoming. This ties into the higher Christ Consciousness, and many in our time have called the I AM as Christ Consciousness. This is not from a religious perspective but from a vibrational frequency; just as Christ was the Son of God, so are you the sons and the daughters of all creation. There is no separation, for God is an expression of you, just as is the Christed One in human form and in great sovereignty. The I AM brings you home and anchors in whatever the truth is that comes next.

This is where you are to be mindFULL. I AM is very powerful, so it is essential that you are using it in service for your highest good and greatest joy. You must use it as a tool for proclaiming and becoming.

I AM can hold a shadow as well. This is evident when you are proclaiming something that you DO NOT wish to be, such as, I am sick, tired, broke, fat, ugly, or any other words that ultimately do not feel good or that you are in fact not willing to be or become.

Words are powerful. Your word is your wand. You may wield it for good or for pain, for creating what you want or more of what you do not want. You choose. What is important is that you are present, aware, pausing, and choosing in accordance with what brings you joy and aligns with what you truly want in each given moment.

Thank You

"If the only prayer you ever say in your entire life is thank you,
it will be enough."

~ Meister Eckhart

These perhaps are the most powerful two words in the English language. In all things, your gratitude is what creates an energy of exchange within the universal frequency. When you say Thank You, you are in fact honoring one of the universal laws of reciprocity. Everything in this human existence is an exchange of energy, everything. Gratitude is one of the most potent energies that anyone can hold in any given moment.

When you find gratitude, you shall find freedom. Thank You can be an illusive phrase as well. It was some years ago when I was with a client who had also become a dear friend, we will call her Mary. As Spirit was graciously whispering through, she was told that at some point her heart would fully forgive the pain of her father who was abusive, dismissive, and unkind to her. Spirit said, "There will be a point in your healing where you will in fact give thanks, perhaps not for the acts he put upon you, but rather for the journey you have walked. Through this journey you have found your voice, your power, strength, and truth. When you find gratitude, you will forever be free of the victimization you are currently experiencing, and your service in the world will be greater for the journey."

Words such as these are potent and often very hard to digest when the pain-body is the loudest voice in the room. Several years later she told me that she was in fact grateful for all she had endured, even though she would not choose such experiences again, she was indeed grateful for the strength, resilience, and true power she came to embody. She was able to sit by his bedside days before he left the physical plane and to indeed set herself free in forgiveness to him.

There is power in gratitude.

Gratitude Practice

Each morning and each night say thank you to three people, things, or experiences you have had or would like to have. Feel the gratitude deeply within your heart and soul. Continue on with this practice each day and express gratitude for three more parts of your life.

LIGHT COUNCIL CHANNEL

"The frequency of you waking up wakes up the entire world, and the expanse of the Universe moves with you, dear one. You have been playing for long enough in the land of the great illusions. The pain and suffering of the old is rapidly falling away.

Be patient with yourself and with the collective at large. In the moments when you feel the isolation of the old limitation, it is in that very moment that your hands reach directly into the heart of the Universe. It is in that moment when you are on your knees, surrendering over tiredness and frailty, that the light reaches back through you to rekindle your heart's flame and carry you home.

It is now, beloved soul, it is now. The old shall fall in its completion, and the new remembered you shall rise in truth and in light. We cannot tell you how. We can only remind you of what getting there feels like, and the rest of your deliverance will be for you to choose.

Choose with your heart and not your head, for if your thinking mind was the key to remembrance, you would have entered the pearly gate of promise, hope, and freedom long ago. Reach within, turn the key, dissolve the old, and let the mystery unravel through you.

We are here in our fullest expression. We are The Light Council, and we serve on high through the light of your soul."

~ The Light Council

Pillar Five
RISE UP

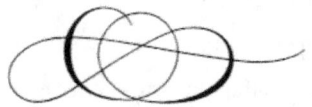

Riding the Dragon

"If you ignore the dragon, it will eat you. If you defy the dragon, it will overpower you. But if you ride the dragon, you will take advantage of its strength and power."

~ Unknown

It had been two and a half months since Tim crossed over. The sheer volume of things I was navigating would put anyone into a complete state of overwhelm. I moved into "do mode" until one day it was done, and there I was. Everyone had gone "home" some time ago. That's the thing with death, one day everyone goes home to the living, and there you are sitting in the void.

My friend Nicole calls and invites me to a four-day retreat in Sedona, and every part of my body says Yes! I need help. I am stuck deeply beneath the heavy blanket of grief and the confusion that comes with it. I know I cannot get up by myself. So, I say, "Yes," buy the ticket, and wait for the time to arrive.

Even landing in Phoenix feels like a rebirth. Travel is my second love language and one of my greatest pleasures. I am met by the most beautiful queen at the airport, a prearranged soul-sister meeting with a woman I had never before met (in this lifetime). Her name is Angel, and she is going to the event as well. And there we are, both in cowboy boots and hats, ready to roll into the great unknown. We jump into her convertible, put the top down, and off we drive to the sacred, healing portal of Sedona, taking Thelma-and-Louise selfies along the way and deeply sharing our hearts through our stories.

The event is filled with magical beings, sacred Kirtan songs, activations, and the raising and riding of the dragon of consciously summoned Kundalini energy. Then the day arrives, the one I am most afraid of and most excited for, the one that is also the reason I had agreed to come. Day three brings us to a deep-dive journey with psilocybin. I had "played" with her in my youth but never as consciously as she demanded, and in return, she kicked my ass several times.

This day, in this conscious well, I welcome her as an ally to support me in rising above the grief beast that had been dancing upon my body, mind, and spirit for almost three months now. Everything is set, the altar perfectly lit, the medicine carefully measured, and the cocoa served ceremonially. Intentions are set, and the two earth medicines are mixed. I drink her in deeply, lie down in the nest I had created, and wait for her magic to unfold.

It doesn't take long. "Oh no, here I go," I think in my head, knowing that I have no resistance, no fight left in me, as I flash back to the previous times when I was taken down the rabbit hole. I pray, "Please be gentle, please work with me, please show me how to transmute this pain, please deliver me home to the light." In that very moment, a beautiful mother-goddess crone is at my feet.

I open my eyes and try to explain. She puts a finger to her mouth to "shhhh" me. Instead of speaking, I look into her eyes. She holds my gaze steady, and without a word, she bows down in honor of me and kisses my feet. I sit up tall, and everything aligns into light. It would be several days later when she would tell me that she saw me struggling to find my power, that Spirit told her I needed to be honored, to be remembered to my high priestess self, and that I was fully present after our connection, fully ready for whatever experience I was to have.

A few hours later I find myself sitting outside of the circle, off to the side, very much alone. The rest of the sixteen participants are at the other end of the room partaking in some deep healings. It is dark now, and the room is brimming with candle light and song, ancient in some way. I pull my white scarf that is wrapped around my shoulders up to my nose and take a deep breath. It smells like home. It smells like the home that is gone, the life that has died. I take another breath. I am spiraling from nostalgia, lost between worlds, and beginning to feel the well of grief rising up within me.

"Please connect me with Tim," I ask. "No," I hear. The grief is pounding in my heart like a freight train. I am slipping so deeply into this pain, and no one sees me. "No one can hold this with me," I say in my heart. "No one can walk this path with me," I say again louder this time. I am weeping uncontrollably, praying that someone can take even a sliver of this pain from me. I, in that moment, like many who have ridden through grief before me, wish that I, too, could die.

Death, I know, is beauty in that moment. Life here in grief is hell. I am falling so deeply into this well of grief that I do not think I will survive. I am praying only that the bottom rises up to meet me soon so that maybe, just maybe, I have a chance to find some steady ground to push off from, so that I can rise up again. I need a push-off point, like sinking to the bottom of the sea and rising back to the surface for a sip of air. "Please let me rise up out of this abyss and find a breath," I ask. It is in that moment when I feel her hand on my heart. I collapse fully into her arms. We say nothing. I weep. She rocks me.

I hear a voice in my heart. I have come, over the years, to call this voice Spirit. Many call it God. I don't think it matters what you call it, as long as you are listening to it. Spirit says, "You can sit here alone swallowed in your grief, your pain, the deep well, the shadow of loss and of longing. Or, you can rise up and walk over there." I look to where the others are gathered. I see the deep medicine and witness the love and support that is collectively unfolding. "You can walk over there," Spirit continues, "and be seen in your healing as you release this pain. You can do this alone or you can do it with support. You choose."

At that moment, I say to my beloved sister, who is still holding my heart, "Thank you. Will you come over there with me so we can be part of the healing?" She agrees, and we stand and walk a few feet across the room. I kneel on my knees right in the middle of it all. My sweet hummingbird friend Nicole, who had invited me, is sitting next to me now. She starts petting me and purring sounds into my ear. "Please stop," I say. She doesn't stop. "NO!" I bark. She immediately pulls back and looks at me with so much love.

In the next moment, I bend over, forehead to floor, and begin to take in the biggest breath I can possibly get into my body. I rise up, and in one motion, like the phoenix rising from the ash, my arms lead and rise way up above my head. My body follows, my head falls back, my mouth cascades open. Then billowing from the depths of my pelvis comes a guttural scream that is, no doubt, heard from miles away. I have no idea what anyone else is doing, nor do I care.

I bend forward again, gathering breath, rising up, and screaming this time from the depth of my soul. The sound curdles in my throat as I squeeze every last drop of breath and sound from my body. All I hear is Larissa, the workshop leader, in front of me, her loving, soft, buttery, angel-wing voice whispering, "Thank you. Thank you, Sister. Thank you for bringing her through. I see you. I love you."

I feel like I have become the dragon beast of grief. She is no longer riding me, I have become her. I AM Kali Ma rising up. I bend again for the third time gathering more fire in my belly, more breath, more power. I rise up tall and howl at the top of my lungs. Out of my mouth surges these words, "She Will Rise!" I shake all of my jewelry, making a loud tambourine sound. My entire body shivers with electric transformation, and in that moment, I bend forward again, this time delivering my forehead to rest upon the earth, and I hand it all over.

In time, I sit up to the gaze of yet another beautiful sister. She looks at me with gentle love and simply asks, "Would you like water?" "Yes, please," I reply. I sip from the cup she's holding up to my mouth, meanwhile the whole crew has moved its attention on to the next holy, otherworldly shift that's taking place. I am free. At that moment I AM Free!

I find out later that the entire room had risen up with me and that their howls were unleashed from the depths of their own beings as well. I had transmuted my grief into power in that moment. I believe in my soul that together we released some of the grief that has been locked deeply within the collective as well.

All of humanity is grieving. As the deconstruction phase is lived through each of your hearts, you are letting go of thoughts, beliefs, emotions, relationships, and people, through distance or death. There is grief for having ever forgotten that you are indeed gods and goddesses in the first place. Grief is a construct of third dimensional living. The journey through density and its intense longing for connection has each of us grieving often.

You are separate from nothing. It is within the banks of your DNA that you will rise up remembered and that you are eternally connected to all things. Even death is but a shift of form. One is never gone, just transmuted. In time, you will see this, and the glory of holding your beloved's energy frequencies will fill and satiate you beyond any moments when longing and grief were once all that you could hold. The time is coming where all shall rise up remembered, connected, whole, and held in love that is unconditional.

Chapter Sixteen
Embrace to Embody

Maybe you are searching among the branches,
for what only appears in the roots.

~ Rumi

We, as humans, are collectively part of the great awakening which is a "coming online," plugging all of us in, like really, truly rebooting the system and coming back online. We have been in a very dark and disconnected slumber for a very, very long time. Asleep at the wheel of life. This disconnection has left humanity operating from a lack of consciousness and a lack of existing in full presence. Opposed to living, there has been more existing, and instead of creating or co-creating with Source itself, humans have been allowing their lives to be created for them, to be imprinted and programmed, with sovereignty being handed over to external forces. Humanity has forgotten that we are the creators and that nothing is ever happening to us but rather always happening through us.

The Light Council says that this intensity, this coming out of the shadow of illusion and darkness, is because all humans must come online, stand in the absolute remembrance of their power, find their souls' connection, and awaken all of their senses.

We are sentient beings, and the volume is turning up so that we have the capacity to see more, to feel more, to intuit more, to move into greater resonance and into truth. It is as if everyone is waking up and becoming their highly sensitive, actualized selves.

This is why everything is holding a more extreme intensity, everything. It doesn't feel like child's play anymore. Everything feels very real, very distorted, extremely important, and often incredibly uncomfortable. In many ways, it is much more than real. This is awakening, and it has an effect upon our every expression.

This is a fundamentally potent moment of transformation where we as humans are literally ushering in a New Earth, the potency of which we cannot begin to fully understand yet. So, whatever the complexities of your own life are, know that it is all for a much larger picture. For now, you can only see through your lens of whatever it is that you are experiencing or feeling. It is easy to attach to the lens of your own reality, but what you actually are doing is a much larger, much grander-scale initiation, activation, and acceleration of creating the New Earth. It's a big deal. You are a big deal!

You've been in the space of embracing concepts, and now let's slide the door open, as you move into this new expression of embodiment. This is time for you to move from conceptual understanding and embracing ideas of "Oh, I get that" to "OH, I AM that."

I've been following and embracing the idea of the Law of Attraction for twenty-five plus years, following Abraham Hicks, and having this notion of how we create from a conceptual space. It makes sense that thoughts become things, that they become things by the reality of thought, which affects the vibration one is holding.

You know this, you have heard it a thousand times. What is available to you now is the embodiment of the principles which create clarity and an understanding of what it actually feels like.

You have now heard me say it many times, 3D or third dimensionality is thought to occur in the mind. It's the thinking mind. Higher resonance 5D or fifth dimensionality or higher is feeling. It is felt within the cells of the body as frequency. It's not "I think I feel." It's "I feel, so I become." The invitation is to move from concepts being embraced to concepts being embodied.

And, how do you get there? Move out of your mind and walk down through your inner staircase to your gut. Sit there in silence until the mind has quieted and you can begin to be in full presence. Say a true statement and feel how your body relaxes into the truth of the statement. Ask yourself some questions. Does the body contract or expand? This is your built-in GPS (God's Positioning System). It lives within your cells, and your body is always communicating the truth to you vibrationally.

There has been so much deconstruction of the principles of manifestation and abundance over the last few years. Many people have marketed it as, "Do you know why the Law of Attraction doesn't work?" It doesn't work because it isn't about saying things one hundred times as affirmations. That is one pathway to get you there, but that alone will never bring you the manifestations you desire. You must get into the feeling state. You create everything by feeling and frequency. Everything on this planet is a frequency, everything. All of it is frequency.

As you are deconstructing the third dimensionality of your thinking mind, your feeling resonance is what is coming online. This is why everything is feeling so heightened and intense. Humanity is coming out of a state of numbness, from only generating and operating from the mind, which holds programs, limitations, ancestral beliefs, and trauma-related expressions. You are moving into the soulular or cellular memory of vibrational frequency. This is where you move into higher dimensionality, becoming one with what you feel and what you feel becoming one with every one of your experiences, your reality.

As you are crossing over the threshold, you are amplifying your senses and sensitivities. You are here reading these words likely because you are a lightworker, a light bearer. You are part of the infusion of light on planet earth that is here to support and elevate the consciousness of the planet. Part of this great awakening is the turning up of the volume on your senses and sensitivities so that you can then be in greater harmony with higher consciousness, higher dimensionality and operate as the embodiment of divine creation.

If you desire for something, then the process becomes one of feeling. You move into feeling something alive within you. This has always been the way. What is different is that it's now more available to you at this moment than it ever has been before. It is in the next breath that you embody YOU as the divine creator and become ONE with everything that you have ever longed to become.

You are in a massive shedding of the old, a tearing away of the confinements of the mind to allow the truest soul expression to find its way through. You are a divine creator. You are an infinite being living in an infinite Universe. The sooner you align with this truth, attaching to the vibrational sequence of this being your truth, the more rapidly your entire life changes.

In the embodiment of the truest understanding of the Law of Attraction, through cellular resonance, so much will change. It's not a concept. It's an expression. The entire Universe comes to life to show you as a gift that moves through you. The second you embody what it is that you desire feels like, you will then see what it looks like with your real eyes.

This embrace to embody is one of the fundamental shifts in dimension hopping. As you are waking up from your sleep to embody the highly sensitive feeling state, everything around you comes to life as well to move into co-creation, into harmony, and into oneness with you. The old way had you suffering in loss, lack, and longing. The new way has you remembering that you would not have a desire for experiencing something if the existence of it was not already alive within you. Wanting is an expression of separation. Feeling relaxed in the presence of the thing within you, even if you do not yet see it, brings you into the full resonance of the Law of Attraction, and everything in the Universe, in that moment, has already transformed to bring the thing into physical form.

So, take a deep breath, relax, and remember. The desire within you is the manifestation of it all into presence.

LIGHT COUNCIL CHANNEL

"You have embraced these concepts for quite some time. It is in your embodiment that you shall be fully remembered as the great creator of your reality. It has always been this, but you had forgotten. In the great remembrance, you shall rise up whole, holy, and in great communion. Whatever you are attaching to outside of yourself for security shall become wobbly.

It is time for you to remember there are only three points of connection that will walk you home to the promised land of your greatest experience of life. Your liberation comes in the connection of self to self, self to higher self, and self to Source itself. When the holy trine of connection is anchored, you shall rise up remembered and in your fullest power. Your manifestations shall be effortless, for the Universe is a splendid playground of infinite possibility that wants nothing more than to bring you everything that you desire.

This is your Spiritual Master's Program. It is in the mastery of remembrance that you shall rise out of the matrix of illusion, the place of lack, loss, separation, and suffering. It is in the embodiment of this remembrance that you will find yourself sovereign and free."

~ The Light Council

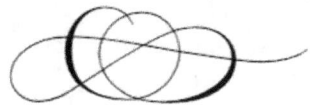

Day of Birth Ritual

"Always accept strange traveling offers.
They are dancing lessons from God."

~ Herman Hesse

It's my birthday. Birthdays are now a huge day of celebration, reflection, ritual, and intention for me. The first birthday I ever celebrated and the first candle I ever blew out to initiate my wish was on my 18th birthday. Birthdays were not a part of my childhood, so I have spent the rest of my life making them count.

This year, I am called to ritualize the journey I have been walking as death opened the gateway of transformation so powerfully within me. My devout wordplay brings me to this birthday to finally realize that ritual is the expression of spi*ritual*. I pray for many days before the big day, asking Spirit how I am to celebrate this cycle. I am already deep into the realization that I had died during this past year, at least a part of me along with so much else I had attached to for identity, safety, and purpose. I had died 100 deaths, only to be reborn 101 times, resurrected really.

I am told that I need to do a release ritual, to let go of that which is complete, to set intentions for what I am willing to receive in the next year, and to set it all free. I know the elements are to be a part of this experience. I am shown that I am to go to the river's edge, gather some twigs and leaves, and make a small raft. I use all biodegradable things because I am very clear that I am to set this raft down the river to meet the sea. I want to set it on fire and watch it move down the river, much like how they put the bodies of the dead upon floating rafts adorned with flowers, light them on fire, and send them down the Thames River.

On the last night of my 52nd year, I light all of the candles on my altar, I pray, clear my energy, and meditate on all that is complete and on all that I am willing to experience during the next trip around the sun. I write it all out on two different sheets of paper. The moon is in its waning phase, much like it was on the night of Tim's death just five months before. I go outside and read the words to the moonlight. As the tears stream from me, I ask with a wavering voice, "Holy Spirit, please take it all from me and leave the lessons so I may use them to serve others in a new way." I light the page on fire and watch it burn in the sacred cauldron I use for magic such as this. I watch until the last spark of light goes poof and all becomes dark.

Next, I pray, "Holy Spirit, please bring me my heart's desires in the best form for me to receive them so that I may use them for my greatest joy and highest service. Thank you, thank you, thank you." I read out loud all the things I am bringing forth and light that paper on fire as well.

It erupts into an inferno ball, and I can't help but understand that my desire for new creation is much bigger than all the pain I had experienced to get me to this point of being ready to receive it all.

I take the ashes from the burned pages of that which is complete and that which is ready to be received and place them in a small container I made out of tissue paper. I also take some of Tim's ashes and mix them together with a fresh cutting of my own hair. I want this ritual to hold our DNA together. The now ash-filled tissue paper is beautifully wrapped with string, and I lay it upon the small float upon a bed of dried red roses from the day of his funeral. I include an owl's feather from one of my ceremonial owl wings, a turkey feather I had once found behind our home, along with a sacred crystal I had had for many, many moons. All beautifully and intentionally created, I place it upon my altar and drift off to sleep.

On the day of my birth, I ask a friend to come to the river with me to witness me. I draw a circle in the sand and set an altar. I welcome the angels and guides, and in that moment, an entire murder of crows (yes, that's what it's called) forms a circle around me. The river is to my front, the ocean to my right and crows are all around squawking at me. I refrain from setting the float on fire as I send it down the river, although that is what I had intended to do. I do not want to be the girl to set California on fire with my death and rebirth ritual. Can you see the headline now?

So off it goes. I watch it float away knowing that, in many ways, I am free to rise up and be reborn in the light of a brand new day, a new year, and a fresh new life.

LIGHT COUNCIL CHANNEL

"Please remember that you are shattering and shifting an entire collective consciousness that has been held in one expression for thousands and thousands of years. It is a magnificent undertaking. You are deconstructing memory banks of pain and suffering that are no longer for you, dearest ones. The complexities of that which is upon you, living and breathing through you, is significant beyond the beyond of everything that you know.

Your hearts and souls are precious, fine-tuned instruments of galactic harmony, and you have only been playing with one, one hundredths of your potential. The breaking down of the old limitation is a journey of reconciliation, the likes of which humanity has never seen. You are doing a magnificent job. Your freedom is alive within you, humming so beautifully alongside the old, outdated program. You call it a breakdown, and we call it a supersonic starseed integration.

We do not care what it is called. We ask only for you to choose in each expression to no longer get stuck in its shadows, but rather rise up in faith, trust, and unity to the light of the brand new day that is revealing itself through you in this moment. There has never been one moment or one experience as potent as this one in which we are meeting with you. A moment such as this has never before occurred and will never again.

This moment, dearest ones, is the moment of your awakening to your ultimate breakthrough, where you tear down the walls of the old and rise to your truest potential and most blinding light.

You are the gods and goddesses of eternity, and your time, master souls, is now. No more is it for you, and shortly no more will it even be available for you, to move into the isolation, the woe, and the worry of the old. You are rising in the remembrance as the Christed One did, and upon your rebirth, the entire galaxy will pivot as you do.

We have said it before and we will say it again and again until you fully hear, until you awaken fully. You are the chosen ones. Your light is greater than any fear that has ever existed. All of this is happening through you, and indeed it is happening for you.

We stand with you this day in awe of your light, holding a mirror to your remembrance and welcoming you home to heaven upon earth. We love you."

~ *The Light Council*

Pillar Six

THE PALACE
OF LIGHT

Chapter Seventeen
Becoming

"A woman in harmony with her spirit is like a river flowing. She goes where she will without pretense and arrives at her destination prepared to be herself and only herself."

~ Maya Angelou

It becomes screamingly obvious, as the days unfold, that part of the ascension is the awakening, harmonization, and rebalance of the Divine Feminine. This is screaming through every cell of my body, as I feel grief begin to release her grip from me. She never goes too far away, but it seems as if each day she is a little less interested in demanding all of my attention. She still enters without knocking and takes whatever she wants, but I seem to be less satisfying to her hunger, less quenching to her thirst each time she comes. With each visit, she seems to stay for less time and makes less of a mess along the way.

"It is my time to RISE," I proclaim, not even sure exactly what that means. I realize I have been asleep for a very long time. A very significant part of me had slipped out the back door when no one was watching. My truest feminine essence is gone, and I am left tired, overweight, uninspired. I feel old and as if I am withering on the vine. I wonder what had happened to me along the way? Where did that spunky, creative, sexy, and playful girl go? Yes, there are all the factors to point a finger at to justify the disappearance: menopause, a long-term relationship, raising a child, supporting a family. Even still, I am too young to feel this old.

Where had my feminine essence gone?

"She's not gone, she's just asleep," my bestie Rachel says, "and you're not washed up, you just haven't been turned on in far too long." I realize at that moment that I have been embodying the masculine in such a strong way that there is no room within me for the feminine principles to be remembered.

It all was imprinted from my youth. My father provided for us, but he didn't know how to care for us. It was never his fault. He was a child of nineteen when he and my mother had me, and his addiction had taken hold years before that.

I have to take a step back and ask, "Do I even know how to be in my truest Divine Feminine form?" The truth is, I have no clue.

The Rise of Ascension

They say that what comes up must come down. I am choosing to flip that on its head. What falls down dies, deconstructs, destroys, and will rise up, in time. It will rise up again, NEW! You are rising up, new. It is the natural order we see in everything. To everything there is a season, turn, turn, turn. After the fall, there is the winter, sometimes the hardest of all seasons. It's the waiting, the wondering, the shivering to the bone that sees nothing but barren branches and dried tumbleweeds. The hibernation, the stillness, the surrender, the full acceptance, the laying yourself down next to the void, knowing that death has indeed occurred. There is a deep knowing within the silence of winter.

Everyone, every living, breathing, or at least vibrating thing knows it, the unspoken truth that keeps everything that moves within the pulse of "life" holding on or in waiting to witness the wonder. The one truth is that within the barren branch is that there is life waiting to show itself again.

Through the awakening, destruction phase, there is a divine knowing that new life is waiting within you to birth. Welcome to the spring. As the clock turns, so does the light of the sun to blast new light upon this earth. It warms the entire sequence, and life begins to emerge, slowly.

It is a constant and ever-changing cycle. You cannot rush the winter to get to the spring. However, your patience will be beautifully honored. As the first glimmers of life emerge, so too shall you rise. New!

The Palace of Light

The journey that unfolded during the time of writing this book has been profound beyond anything I could have ever imagined.

With so much movement and uncertainty, it has been a journey of presence, surrender, allowing, and trust at levels I had never perceived as possible. Door after door closing, another house selling from under me, directing yet another move, one year to the day. "You just need the next steps," Spirit said over and over, as I found myself too often on the floor, on my knees, in puddles of tears, begging to be shown where I was to go, "Where, oh where, is my Palace of Light?"

Looking at the few remaining boxes to be unpacked, holding some of my most sacred objects that I have not touched in over a year, I have arrived. The light of the dawn is casting its yellow glow through the french doors, just beyond my writing table. The scent of coffee and incense blending with the wet red clay and desert grasses of the high desert has my senses dizzied. Halo, my cat, is enjoying watching the world wake up comfortably behind the safety of the screen, as the coyotes howl in the distance.

This is home, at least for now. Sedona has summoned me into her magic with the one door that opened so wide that, no matter how much I resisted, I had to walk through it. I cannot deny the beauty that is all around me, from the land with its red glowing earth to the mountains catching the light of the most expansive, dramatic, constantly changing skies. Every day is new, just like me. Every day I wake up with the rebirth of this dark night of the soul's journey taking shape within me. I often ask, "Who am I now?"

Is this my Palace of Light? I wonder, as I cannot help but acknowledge that there is only soft and subtle light gently pouring into this home, very typical for Arizona homes, to help with the months of intense heat. I long for the cascading of light and phenomenal views I have become accustomed to in the search for a Palace of Light. I take pause with curiosity. I know in my heart I am here for a reason or a season, and it will be clear, in time.

There is nothing like a Sedona night with its dark city and full explosion of stars. The sky is a crescendo of magic. I find myself with a sweet gathering of friends and am delighted by the orchestra of crickets, the deep hoot of a far-away owl, and the sound of cicadas taking over the evening. It is at this moment when I look toward my home all aglow from the inside out. The house is pulsating with a soft amber rose light that feels as if it is pouring outward through every window.

A large star of gold shines above the front door. I take it in for a very long time. My neighbor Robert asks, "Are you alright?" as tears fill the edges of my eyes and begin to gently create a stream of sweet, salty flow down my face. I realize in this moment that I have indeed found my next Palace of Light. For this palace, I had to journey through the darkness of night to find my way home. This palace glows as a beacon through the darkness, from the inside out, warm, comforting, like the womb of a divine mother welcoming me home.

I remember in this moment that the Palace of Light lives eternal within each of us. It has been here all along. I laid in wait for the sun, some higher expression of self, or God to pour the light through to me, but in truth, it is in the darkness that the pure light of our inner expression can shine freely forth. When that light is awakened, cast freely in its greatest expression, its light pours forth endlessly in every direction.

The Palace of Light is within you. In your natural awakened state, it shines forth, and all any of us are truly ever doing is walking each other home to the remembrance of this one powerful and profound truth.

Epilogue

I am the Red Phoenix!

I rose up fierce from the ash after the inferno came and burned the entirety of everything to the ground.

I tried to stop it with my bare hands, holding the essence of the Divine Mother deep within my womb, but even she backed up so that death could walk in.

I tried to save the pieces in tucked away boxes high above the roof line. I tried to save the children that hid curled up behind the doors. I tried to pick the fruit and all of the flowers before they chopped down the trees and pulled up the roots, the scent of cherries and roses lingering still in the air just above the leveled dirt.

I tried to house the kitten that could only run free, lost, and alone, hiding behind the tomatoes left growing like wild weeds, until the day my beloved took her with him to the other world.

And as I laid myself down, as the flames licked through me, devouring every drop of my nectar, dried and barren, I died. The moss was rolled over me, and darkness was all I could see.

Until the day came when the earth peeled back, and the stones rolled, and she rose up. She was fierce with a dragon's head and a woman's heart, burning as a new fire was birthed within her. She sprinkled magic upon the land and watched it spring to new life.

"You cannot rush the winter, dear one," she was told. When the bloom comes, it is memorable beyond anything ever before known. The beauty that pours forth takes the breath of even the most stoic.

This is how worlds are formed. Her magic dripped through the center of Gaia and together they rose, womb to womb, dropping petals of faraway scents, elixirs to the weary and the wild of heart.

"She Will Rise!" was screamed for all to hear, and in time, it has been made true!

I AM the Red Phoenix, and in the wake of my fury and my love, all shall rise with me, liberated, remembered, and free.

~ Lisa McCardle

Acknowledgements

Thank you, dearest friends and family, too many to name, for walking me through the hard days, the dark nights, always offering light along my path as I found my way home. Thank you for celebrating each win, for your endless love and belief in me, and the path forward. Thank you, Plasha and Randy Will for being there for so many beginnings and endings, for being my family and my first phone call in my moments of need. Thank you, Sarah Keruish, for seeing me, for your neverending belief in this book, and for your patience and loving encouragement along the way. Suzi Liz for the years of endless support with my mission on the planet and for fine-tuning the words of this book. Maya, Karrine, and the Giamona family for being our family. Shawna Garritson and Jen Nobles for the countless hours of presence, patients, love and support. Jen and Russel Peevey for loving us through and through. Rochelle Bartholomew for your unwavering presence. Jennifer Rosenthal for your wisdom when we needed it most. Leah Rowe for the walk through life and grief neither of us thought we would journey together. Jen DeVilliers for holding me. Nicole and Aram Stoney for your continued love and support. Thank you, Andrea Billig, for the guidance in bringing this book to print. Thank you to all who have touched both these pages and my heart in all of the profound and memorable ways. Thank You. Thank You. Thank You.

About The Author

LISA MCCARDLE

Creator of Inner Wisdom Awakening, Lisa McCardle is an Author, Award-winning Speaker, Quantum Energy Healer, Transformational Life Coach, Spiritual Teacher, and Light Council Channel. For nearly thirty years, Lisa has guided high-powered female executives, influencers, and everyday people through the process of awakening for expansion, finding true purpose, and reclaiming personal power, the feminine way. She is passionate about supporting souls in plugging back into the source from which they were created, so they may awaken to their fullest potential and watch the magic of their extraordinary lives unfold before them.

Through the death/rebirth journey shared in these pages, she has awakened in remembrance to the power of the Priestess Pathway that she is anchoring more strongly to each day. She is supporting the rise of the Feminine through the ancient temple arts practices and awakening the SHE (Sacred Hearts Emergence) Movement. She will be launching her next book, The Many Faces of Mary, in the spring of 2024, where she will walk you through the great remembrance and reclamation of the truth of the Divine Feminine awakening journey.

Lisa would love to walk with you home to your greatest sight, balanced feminine power, and most abundant life.

To connect with Lisa, please scan this QR Code.

She Power Portal

SHE **Power Portal** is a monthly membership that supports you to stay connected to Yourself, Higher Self, and Source itself. This growing community of Women gathers together for love, support, elevation, and spiritual alchemy. We no longer need to walk this path alone. There are three levels to meet your needs and keep you connected along your journey of ascension.

https://lisamccardle.com/portal/

www.ingramcontent.com/pod-product-compliance
Lightning Source LLC
Chambersburg PA
CBHW071155130626
46553CB00004B/1668